ANIMAL KIND

ANIMAL KIND

Lessons on Love, Fear and Friendship

from the Animals in Our Lives

BY EMMA LOCK

CORAL GABLES

Published by Mango Publishing Group, a division of Mango Media Inc.

Cover Design: Elina Diaz
Cover Photo/illustration: Christin Lola/Shutterstock
Layout & Design: Elina Diaz

For permission requests, please contact the publisher at:
Mango Publishing Group
2850 S Douglas Road, 2nd Floor
Coral Gables, FL 33134 USA
info@mango.bz

For special orders, quantity sales, course adoptions and corporate sales, please email the publisher at sales@mango.bz. For trade and wholesale sales, please contact Ingram Publisher Services at customer.service@ingramcontent.com or +1.800.509.4887.

Animal Kind: Lessons on Love, Fear and Friendship from the Animals in Our Lives

Library of Congress Cataloging-in-Publication number: 2019948623
ISBN: (print) 978-1-64250-162-9, (ebook) 978-1-64250-163-6
BISAC category code PETS / Essays & Narratives

Printed in the United States of America

For those who keep me safe,
but leave me wild.

Table of Contents

INTRODUCTION

I'm fairly confident that most fledgling authors don't normally type "How to write a book introduction" into their Google search bar. I'm also mostly convinced that other writers' search histories don't include terms like "What if my book doesn't sell?," "Dealing with imposter syndrome" and "Should I just give up on my life, bury myself in the cold soil, and become a carrot?"

The truth is that as much as I have yearned to write this book and have been utterly and completely obsessed with this project for months, this book almost didn't happen.

It's exciting to enter into a project where you know that you will be baring your soul (with all its sparkles and shadows) on paper or in an audiobook for the first time, but there's also something unexpectedly jarring about it too. It's a surreal feeling to know that the words you write, the lessons you learn, and the secrets you share may be enjoyed, critiqued, or survive for many decades. That is, unless this book becomes the disgrace of all literature and a secret, elite band of authors issue an order to have all copies of this book burned.

I think I've finally made peace with the fact that the circumstances under which I finished writing *Animal Kind* have been less than ideal. Indeed, my imposter syndrome and self-doubt have paled into insignificance when I think back over the past three months and wonder how on earth I managed to survive what can only be described as an unexpectedly prolonged nightmare.

In my personal story "Bear," which you will read a little further into the book, you will glimpse a world which I have kept hidden and ferociously protected for several years. There is a part of me, though it is much less dominant now, which didn't want to share this part of my story, worried that I might be viewed as damaged goods or somehow a failure.

The truth is that everyone has their struggles. Nobody could (or should) journey through life without picking up a few bumps and bruises here and there.

In a way, we're a bit like bananas. We start off a little green and rather sweet, but rapidly become less firm (well, hello there, thirties!) and we begin to accumulate bruises and blemishes which make us unique. If you take away anything from this book, it's that we are all bananas.

When I first put pen to paper (or rather fingers to phone) I was cruising at about 33,000 feet on a flight to Omaha,

Nebraska, eager to finally collect my long awaited Eurasier puppy, Kiba. If you're unfamiliar with the Eurasier as a breed, they resemble a colourful Samoyed and can be found in stunning wolf-grey colours, reds, agoutis, and all black. Kiba is almost completely a solid black colour, with a little secret patch of red armpit hair. He might bless you with a glimpse of these magical hairs if you give him a belly rub. They've simply been developed as a companion breed, even-tempered and fabulous-looking.

I was inspired to begin writing *Animal Kind* at this time because a few seats ahead of me on the aircraft was a man and his service dog—a beautiful border collie.

Knowing that I had been given the green light to begin writing my book about the ways in which animals inspire positive change in our lives, and knowing now that Kiba had been selected from his litter to become my ESA, I felt that the timing was right.

If you're unfamiliar with the term "ESA" it stands for "Emotional Support Animal." In North America, Emotional Support Animals, Therapy Animals, and Service Animals provide invaluable services.

Therapy Animals have a calm, sweet demeanour and bring joy to many people by visiting them in hospitals, care homes, and special needs schools. They are also sometimes present in police interview rooms to comfort young witnesses and victims of crime.

Service Animals are highly trained and highly skilled animals who perform duties and tasks for their disabled owners. Seeing-eye dogs are probably the most widely recognised Service Animals, but other types of service animal can include "medical alert" dogs trained specially to detect seizures or remind their humans to take their medications. Other Service Animals perform tasks which aid their owners, such as opening and closing doors, learning to dial 911 in an emergency, or grounding their owner during a PTSD attack.

Service Animals are most typically dogs but can be miniature horses as well. It is current US law that Service Animals have public access, meaning that they are generally permitted to accompany their owners anywhere a human is permitted to be, such as on aircrafts, at the movie theatre, in restaurants, and in shopping malls. Yes, this means that, on occasion, miniature horses accompany their owners on flights. It's the most bizarre, but adorable sight.

Service Animals are not considered "pets." They are considered to be medical equipment, and therefore necessary to be present with their owners.

Emotional Support Animals are not required to be highly trained or highly skilled animals, and their owners don't always have a disability. Therefore ESAs are not Service Animals, but they do offer invaluable therapeutic benefit to their owners by offering comfort and companionship. Emotional Support Animals can technically be any pet (yes, even bullfrogs can be ESAs) but only emotional support dogs (and sometimes cats) are permitted to fly in the cabin of an aircraft if they're well behaved. Emotional Support Animals are not classified as medical equipment and therefore do not automatically have public access rights.

On my flight to collect Kiba, I was so excited that I hadn't realised that I was practically vibrating. I was shaking my leg, sighing, fidgeting and glancing down at my watch every few minutes. The air hostess who came to offer me a beverage picked up on my body language and asked if I was a nervous flyer. We both laughed when I told her that I was actually just very excited to be meeting my puppy when we landed.

After sipping on some ginger ale (my favourite drink), I put on my huge headphones which are shaped like cat ears and listened to one of my favourite albums, *Levity* by Dax Johnson.

I began to write down some of my ideas for the book and channelled my restless pre-puppy excitement into a general outline for my personal story, "Bear."

This book is intended to be a celebration of the meaningful bonds and relationships humans and animals can form and to pay homage to the many varied ways in which animals help us in our daily lives.

As no two people or animals are alike, neither are these chapters. Each short story is its own entity, inspired by the real friendships, discoveries, and undeniable love between the human protagonist and the animals in their lives.

In the case of the short stories "Buddy," "Zak," "Magic," and "Bubbles," I have written adaptations of these true stories based on my conversations with their generous contributors. However, in the case of "Bear," I have chosen to write my story factually as I remember it. No detail is altered or embellished. The chapter is written as accurately as I can remember, which makes the story a colossal tidal wave of emotion and distress. My hopes are that the chapters reflect the truth of who I am, affected by such a disorder and experiencing total free-fall. Perhaps some readers will be able to relate. If you can, I see you. I acknowledge your struggle, and you're doing great.

At the end of each chapter, I've compiled a short list of fascinating facts about the species of animal featured in the story, as well as shared pictures of the real animals and humans who inspired that chapter.

My hope is that in sharing these pictures with the reader, we can visually enjoy how such different animals have made monumental and surprising impacts, and that we can, in a small way, immortalize and honour them.

This book has been a true labour of love and a journey which has forced me to rise above the challenges I have faced in my personal life to complete this project. In completing *Animal Kind*, I have proved to myself that I am not defined by my disorder, and that it does not hold infinite power over me. In this exact moment, at 12:15 p.m. on an otherwise uneventful Wednesday in the middle-of-nowhere New Jersey, I feel quite proud of myself. It's a feeling I'm trying to feel more often.

In truth, the greatest daily support, motivator, and reason to get out of bed each morning has been Kiba. As I have written *Animal Kind*, he has transformed from being a football-sized, clumsy ball of fluff under my writing desk to a huge, majestic bear-wolf with eyes that hold more wisdom and love than I can express. He has become my shadow, protector, fluffy shoulders to cry on, and best friend.

When I first set out to write this book, I wanted to open people's eyes to the magic of human-animal relationships and to share how deeply profound they can be. It is, in a way, poetic, and just right, that the reason this book has finally come to fruition has been because of a new story of friendship which is organically writing itself every day, born of love, trust, cubes of cheese, and belly rubs.

ZAK

A sharp crack followed by a dull thud woke Heather from her sleep. Deep from within the many cozy layers of blankets hugging the bed came a startled, almost cough-like "woof."

Heather squinted through the darkness at her motionless bedroom and shimmied herself into a sitting position in bed, her heart still beating hard from being awoken suddenly. She stretched her arm out into the chilly air, reached for the switch on her bedside table, and clicked on the light. The room immediately illuminated with a soft, warm yellow glow.

Looking left and right, Heather scanned her bedroom. Her chair was still piled high with the laundry she had been meaning to put away. Her bookshelf was a shabby-chic assortment of books, eclectic ornaments, and picture frames. Nothing was out of place or showed any sign of disturbance.

She reached for her phone and squinted as its harsh white light assaulted her tired eyes. It was only 4:45 a.m.

Under her duvet, a small, pillow-sized lump began to wriggle its way up her legs, hips, and stomach. Heather glanced down as her blankets rose up like a small hill and fell back to reveal the inquisitive face of her Staffordshire Bull Terrier, Zak.

 For a Staffordshire Bull Terrier, or "Staffie," as they're affectionately referred to by dog lovers, Zak was dainty for his breed. His short, wiry coat, once a rich fawn colour, was now heavily flecked with white and grey. Over the past thirteen years, age had slowly crept up on Zak. What had started out as just a few white whiskers on his chin and muzzle had multiplied, migrating upwards and steadily turning his entire face white. The years had also added silky white socks to his paws, which perfectly matched his distinguished face.

"Hi, boy," whispered Heather as she gave Zak a quick scratch under his chin. He narrowed his eyes in quiet enjoyment.

Still curious about the sound which woke her, Heather swung her legs out of bed and hastily tucked her feet into the fluffy pink novelty slippers her mother had given her for Christmas a few weeks earlier. Zak hopped onto the floor and shook his little body, the clinking of his collar and tags filling the room with familiar sound.

Heather stood up and tensed slightly as the chilly air brushed against her body, sending an uncomfortable shiver down her back. She reached toward her chair and peeled her freshly washed house robe from the pile, quickly wrapping its plush fabric around her body and fastening it tightly.

Heather shuffled to the window by her bed, pulled back the dark, heavy curtains, and peered out into the night. What had been a light peppering of powdery snow when she had gone to sleep was now a luxurious blanket of snow and ice covering the rolling Scottish hills which her home was nestled in. Heather noticed that an old branch had broken away from the rowan tree right outside her bedroom window and was now on the ground, disappearing quickly under the cotton ball-sized snowflakes falling from the sky.

Satisfied that she had found the source of the noise, she glanced down to her side at Zak. He was standing as high up on his hind legs as possible, his front paws resting on the windowsill. His huge black nose was pressed against the window, and his warm exhalations were fogging up the glass as he looked out excitedly at the monochrome landscape.

Although time had noticeably changed Zak over the years, his playful energy had never waned, and he still moved with the ease and speed of a much younger dog.

"Forget about it," said Heather playfully as she drew the curtains shut once again and gestured for Zak to get down. "We'd both catch our deaths."

Zak gave a defiant snort and trotted over to the bedroom
door. He sniffed at the small crack under the door and
purposefully sat down, appealing to Heather with his large,
brown eyes.

"Great," thought Heather, wishing to go back to bed. She
glanced at her phone one more time, sighed, and walked
over to her bedroom door, cracking it slightly to allow Zak
through first.

Heather yawned and wiggled her toes to keep them warm as
she filled the kettle with water and set it on its base to boil.
Zak busied himself with his routine of sniffing the kitchen
floor for any crumbs or delicious morsels of food which may
have evaded the dustpan and brush. He pawed under the
oven and pulled from beneath it a forgotten pig's ear chew.
Heather chuckled to herself as Zak proudly strutted to the
living room with his dust-covered prize. He jumped up onto
the sofa and circled twice before he plopped his body down
and began inspecting his chew.

Heather sprinkled some chai leaves into her favourite green
teapot and slowly added the boiling water, enjoying how the
tea leaves swirled and began to change the colour of the
water. Glancing up at the window above the sink, she could
see that the snow was still falling heavily. Her thoughts

turned to her day ahead, and she considered which route would be the best for her to drive to work.

She poured some of the chai tea into a mug and took a long, warming sip.

Having lost interest in his chew, which was now on the floor, Zak had instead turned his attention to chasing his tail, his soft, round mouth reaching back over his body to capture the most elusive of his limbs. Heather watched as her senior dog trampled her sofa cushions and caught a glimpse of his aged and discoloured teeth—teeth which she had been so afraid of as a child.

Heather crossed the kitchen into the living room and settled onto the plush sofa next to Zak. He was now clumsily slumped over on his side, mouthing one of his back feet, having given up on his tail.

"Come here, you marshmallow!" sighed Heather, patting her free hand on her thigh.

Zak heaved his compact body up and plonked himself against her lap. He rested his heavy head on her knee and let out a long exhalation—the kind some might think of as a sign of boredom, but in reality was blissful contentment. Heather stroked his silky triangular ears and raised her teacup to her mouth as her eyes shifted focus to a picture frame perched on the windowsill. It was an old, cherished photo which showed her mother, father, brother, and herself as a young girl. Her gaze rested on the cheeky grin of her father's face. She missed him every day, but the holidays were always especially difficult. She closed her eyes and tried her best to remember the sound of his voice and his infectious laughter.

As a child, Heather had mostly lived under the firm but fair rule of her mother, Joan, a capable, no-nonsense kind of woman who, with a single raised eyebrow or lash of her sharp tongue, could make the toughest Scotsman cower in fear. Although she was a formidable woman, she was always a tender and nurturing mother to her two children and expertly handled all of her roles as the primary carer, breadwinner, and disciplinarian in their small family home. Heather's father, Steve, was a kind and lively man. Beloved by many, he was always the life and soul of a party. Despite the deep age lines etched on his face, it wasn't hard to see that, in his youth, Steve would have made all of the women in town weak at the knees.

Although Steve was as warm and loving as a father could be, his body had begun to suffer irrevocably from the effects of liver disease, and both he and Joan had decided that it would be kindest to their children if he were to move back into his mother's home, which was only a short distance away.

Despite living away from their father during the week,
neither Heather nor her younger brother Thomas noticed
that their family was any different from anyone else's. On
the weekends, their mother would dress them in their best
sweaters, and together the three of them would walk the short
distance to their grandmother's house to visit their father.
He would always swing open the front door enthusiastically,
and welcome Heather and her brother with huge bear hugs
and lots of kisses. They'd enjoy their time together, kicking
footballs around the garden and playing games of hide-and-
seek. Their grandmother would cook the most delicious roast
dinners with Yorkshire puddings, and after supper they'd
each pick out a sweet treat and cuddle up on the sofa to
watch a Disney film.

This familiar, comforting routine would faithfully repeat
itself every week, come rain, shine, or snow, but as the
seasons passed and Heather grew to become more curious
and aware of the world around her, she began to notice a
change in her father.

During their weekend visits, their grandmother would often
become the smiling face to greet them at the door when they
arrived. Their father wouldn't want to play outdoors as much,
and some weeks, Heather would notice that he would wear
the same clothes, or wouldn't have shaved his face, making
him appear frighteningly aged. His jokes and laughter

became distant memories, lost in happier times, and,
increasingly, Heather would be encouraged by her mother to
have weekend sleepovers with her friends, or to spend more
time with other family members.

One Saturday morning, Joan sat down with Heather and
Thomas and softly explained to them that their father had
been feeling extremely low which was why they hadn't been
able to see as much of him lately. Heather nodded dutifully
as her mother expressed how she felt he might benefit from
having some more constant company such as a dog or cat.
That very afternoon, Heather, along with her mother and
brother, drove the short distance to the local dog rescue to
find a suitable pet for their father.

The dog viewing room was frighteningly loud and filled with
dogs of all shapes, colours, and sizes. Some of adoptable dogs
had extensive notes and background information attached
to the clipboards which hung on the outside of their pens.
Others simply had pieces of paper with the words "Adopted,"
or "Undergoing Evaluation" scribbled on.

Heather felt a pang of sorrow as she passed a pen containing
a huge, emaciated-looking German Shepherd, and another
pen containing an assortment of Jack Russell terriers,
Chihuahua mixes, and a small, tear-stained Shih Tzu with a
snaggle tooth.

"Aww! This one is so cute and looks so sad, Mummy," whined Heather as she crouched down and extended her small fingers through the bars of the pen. Immediately, the tiny Shih Tzu let out an ear-splitting shriek and bolted toward the back of the pen. It hid beneath one of the elevated dog beds where it continued to yowl, sending the rest of its cage-mates into an excited frenzy of barking and jumping. Heather stumbled backward in fright and clung to her mother's coat.

"That's not the right dog for you," came the deep voice of a kennel technician from inside another pen. "She's not good around children. She's going to need a very quiet, experienced home to help her with her confidence."

Heather felt her mother's firm, reassuring hand grasp her shoulder, and together they continued along the rows of home-seeking dogs.

"Hey! What about this one?" came Thomas's voice from the far end of the viewing room.

At the back of the pen was a small, fawn-coloured Staffordshire Bull Terrier with ears that resembled crumpled autumn leaves. His brown, expressive eyes were alert, but friendly, and as Heather and Joan approached, he stood up from his bed, stretched, and bounded toward the front of the pen to greet them enthusiastically.

Thomas stuck his little hand into the enclosure, and the
chubby puppy licked and mouthed his hand gently while
pawing at his sleeve.

"Now that's a great dog for you," said the kennel technician
brightly as he came over to join them. "He was found as
a stray, but he's very friendly. He's young, so he's very
trainable, and he tested safe around children and other dogs.
He's a Staffordshire Bull Terrier, but don't let the 'Bull' part
put you off. Staffies are great family dogs and can adapt to
almost any lifestyle."

Heather scrunched her face up as both her mother and
brother fawned over the energetic puppy. She was unnerved
at the sight of the huge, toothy grin the dog seemed to
be giving.

"Daddy, daddy! We got you a present!" exclaimed Thomas
as he and his mother carried Zak's crate and a bag of pet
supplies into the house.

Heather watched quietly from the safety of the sofa as the
boisterous puppy zoomed around the living and bulldozed
into her grandmother's the coffee table. The puppy, now
named "Zak" was tearing around the entire first floor of the
house, mouthing everything he encountered and performing
exaggerated play-bows, appealing for someone to engage

him in play. She looked over at her father, his gaze focused entirely on his unexpected, hyperactive gift. She watched in silent hope as the faintest ghost of a smile formed on her father's face.

Almost immediately, Steve and Zak became inseparable companions. Zak provided Heather's father with some much-needed comfort, and his need for daily walks encouraged Steve to make more of an effort to get up each morning and head out of the front door. Having a dog turned out to be a great way to engage in light conversation with strangers, and both Heather and Thomas noticed that visits to their father's house were much more cheerful than they had been in months. He had even started to shave again.

During the fleeting summer months, Heather would look forward to the weeklong camping trips she took with her mother's family. Sadly, her father was never quite well enough to join in the fun, but being bundled together in caravan with her favourite cousins and doting aunties and uncles were the holidays Heather looked forward to the most. This summer, the whole family had chosen to explore the beautiful Lake District in the north of England. The Lake District is famous for its rugged beauty, its untamed expanse of ancient woodland and forest, and of course its stunning, seemingly endless sapphire blue lakes.

For a whole week, Heather scarcely had a moment to rest.
Her days were full of laughter as she hiked, fished, and
giggled with her cousins as they swapped secrets. By night,
everyone would huddle around the campfire in their pyjamas
and drink hot chocolate with marshmallows as the uncles
and older cousins took turns sharing ghost stories and spine-
chilling urban legends. By the time Heather's head hit the
pillow each night, she was already sound asleep, peacefully
dreaming of the previous day's fun and anticipating the
promise of more sunshine adventures to come.

"Heather?"

From her deep sleep, Heather could hear someone
calling her name.

"Heather, wake up, love."

She cracked her sleep-filled eyes open just the tiniest amount
and groaned as the morning light poured into her eyes. She
could just about make out the silhouette of her mother. For
a moment, she thought that she might be dreaming, but her
mother spoke again.

"You need to wake up and pack your things, love. We have
to leave."

Heather rubbed her eyes and sat up in her air mattress. Looking around, she could see that her cousins were all still asleep, peacefully snoring under many mismatched blankets and duvets.

"W-why? What's wrong?" she croaked.

"It's your father" her mother whispered. "He's taken a turn for the worse and we have to go to him straight away."

The guttural sound of the car rang in Heather's ears as they raced back up the motorway toward Glasgow. A cold numbness descended on Heather as they tried desperately to make their way to the hospital. Vaguely, she could hear her mother trying to calm Thomas down, so, to spare her mother's feelings, Heather held back her own tears and asked no questions. She allowed her mind to shift into autopilot as she silently hoped and prayed that she was somehow having a bad dream.

She did not notice her mother furiously shouting at the security guard who protested her parking the car in a reserved space. She did not feel her legs moving as they ran up the stairs of the car park and sprinted toward the hospital reception doors. She could hardly register the words of the nurse who ushered them through the labyrinth of sterile corridors and bleak waiting areas.

Not until they reached a private room, where a sombre looking surgeon was waiting outside for them, did Heather finally realise that she was not dreaming. Her heart shattered as the sound of her mother's distraught cries pierced her mental fog and brought her back to reality.

Whether a minute or an hour had passed, Heather did not know. She looked up at her mother, who was crying into the surgeon's shoulder, and then she glanced down at Thomas. His large, watery eyes and lost expression awoke a strength in Heather which she hadn't known before. She silently vowed that she would be strong for her family as she held her brother and hugged her mother.

The funeral passed by in a blur of flowers and familiar faces. Heather stayed true to her promise. She bit her lip as the coffin bearers carried her father's casket into the church, and she held her chin up as family members cupped her shoulder and told her to be strong. The summer sun did little to warm Heather or lift her spirits, but she valiantly tried to continue on with an air of normalcy for the sake of everyone around her.

A week after the funeral, Heather awoke to find her mother and grandmother having coffee and cake in the kitchen. She could tell from their red noses and the abundance of tissues on the table that they had been crying, so she greeted her grandmother with a smile and as much warmth as she could possibly muster. As she hugged her grandmother, Heather heard a small whimper, and she glanced down to see Zak in his pet carrier.

"Your father left him to you," said her grandmother.

Heather was stunned into silence. Her mother smiled and nodded at her in an encouraging manner. Crouching down onto her knees, Heather peered into the carrier at the lost-looking puppy. He seemed depressed, his sad eyes accentuated by how flat his ears were lying against his head. Although she liked Zak, she only saw him on her weekend visits to her dad's house, and she was secretly still afraid of his energy and his habit of putting his huge mouth around everything he could fit in it.

Joan could sense her daughter's hesitation.

"It's alright if you don't want to take him, Heather. We can find him a good home somewhere else." Almost as though Zak could understand their conversation, he whined softly and licked at the grate of his carrier.

Heather peered over at her grandmother. Although she had been caring for her father, she, too, was in poor health and couldn't possibly take care of such an energetic puppy.

"Can we try for a week?" asked Heather.

Her mother nodded in agreement and opened the carrier to allow Zak out to explore his new home.

Suddenly having to adjust to having Zak at home was not easy. He was teething, and, like many teething puppies, he liked to chase legs and feet as they walked past. At bedtime, Zak would not settle on the floor and would whine and cry out in the darkness.

Toward the end of their weeklong trial of having Zak at home, Heather was just about to drift off to sleep in her bed. Suddenly Zak's needle-sharp puppy teeth nipped up at her toes, piercing her sock and nicking her skin.

"Owch, Zak! No!" cried Heather in a mixture of anger and pain, and she scrambled quickly up the bunkbed ladder into Thomas's bed.

Being a heavy sleeper, Thomas did not stir, but Heather couldn't get comfortable. It was far too hot to be sharing a bed, and she didn't want to climb back down to her bed and risk another bite to her feet.

Over an hour passed, and Heather was growing increasingly warm and uncomfortable. She peered over the side of the top bunk. Her bedroom door was cracked ever so slightly open, the light from the hallway gently illuminating a patch of carpet on the floor and the small brown lump that was Zak. Heather's mind wandered back to her grandmother's house and how her father always enjoyed telling everyone how Zak loved to cuddle up at night. How was it possible to cuddle something so annoying and with such sharp teeth? Did her father really bond with Zak that much?

Carefully, so as not to wake Thomas or Zak, Heather pulled herself over the side of the top bunk and slowly placed her foot on the wooden ladder. Zak immediately lifted his head and watched silently, his head tilting from side to side as Heather slowly descended and, without touching floor, climbed back into her bed.

Scarcely a moment had passed before she felt the telltale signs of Zak trying to climb up on her bed once more. She curled her toes, anticipating the sharp pain of Zak's needle-sharp teeth once more.

The mattress dipped slightly as the puppy used all of his upper body strength to heave himself up onto the bed. Heather held her breath as she watched him disappear under the duvet where her feet would normally be and silently began to panic as Zak began to belly crawl under the covers, up over her knees, past her hips and up toward her chest. A moment later, the duvet rose up by her neck and fell backward to reveal Zak's huge, smiling face. His smooth, round liquorice nose was touching her own. Each time she breathed in, she inhaled his light, comforting scent. A scent which she had often faintly smelled on her father. Without warning, Heather felt her eyes begin to prickle. She had tried so hard to be strong for her family, but lying in the darkness with her father's familiar scent floating around her, she finally dropped her guard and allowed herself to cry. Like a warm summer rain, the tears began to fall, leaving salty, wet trails on her cheeks. With each tear, stifled sob, and grit of her teeth, Zak gently licked her cheeks and ear, laying his body on her chest, his warm weight comforting her. His eyes were gentle and full of understanding, almost as if to say, "I miss him too."

***

The distant rumble of snowploughs startled Heather. Scattered in the distance, the headlights of cars reflected off of the snow, casting eerie shadows over the hills. Had she fallen back asleep? She glanced outside. It had stopped snowing.

Heather had was still absentmindedly holding her mug of chai tea in her hand, though now it was lukewarm, and its sweet aroma had dissipated.

Nestled against her thigh, Zak stared up at her lovingly with his dark, cacao bean eyes. He licked his lips contentedly as she gently kneaded and massaged his greying scruff.

Less than twenty minutes later, Heather, now bundled in copious amounts of warm layers, complete with snow boots, a thick scarf, and earmuffs, was blasting the heat in her car as high as it would go. The snow melted off her ice scraper and was creating a sludgy puddle of water on the floor in front of the passenger's seat.

Heather's phone chimed once and a message from one of her colleagues lit up its screen: "Hi H.! Someone just dumped a box of Staffie puppies outside the shelter. Could really use some reinforcements. Drive safe, the roads are mad!"

Heather secured her phone back into its dashboard cradle and looked out at Zak. His robust body was protected from the cold by a Christmas-themed dog sweater she had dressed him in. He was panting hard from having galloped at full speed through the driveway snow, his hot breath turning the air around him into mist.

"Are you coming, then?" she called as she opened
her car door.

In one bound, Zak enthusiastically leapt into the car and
onto the passenger-side seat where he immediately settled
himself into a ball shape. With his red and green sweater,
he almost resembled a Christmas pudding. She smiled at
his willingness to follow her wherever she went, and she
wondered if he was aware that the dog rescue she now
managed was the same place they had first met all those
years ago.

As she carefully steered her way through the snowy
landscape, she thought of her family and how they had
built snowmen together, her father lifting her up onto
his shoulders so that she could place the carrot on the
snowman's face.

She would always miss and yearn for her father, but, in many
ways, she felt that he was never truly gone, having left behind
a most precious Staffordshire Bull Terrier to love and protect
her. Zak had walked faithfully by her side as she grew out of
her overalls and into makeup. He watched proudly from the
sidelines as she tore open the envelope containing her exam
results and both she and her mother jumped and cried out
with joy. And when the hard day finally came for Heather
to leave the safety of her family's nest and grow in her own

space, Zak was sitting by her side as the real estate agent handed her the keys to her home.

 Zak was the most wonderful and comforting gift her father could ever have left for her, and she would be forever grateful to him for the love and lessons he taught her in their short time together. Above all, she loved him for having the wisdom to leave her with the greatest gift of all, unconditional love.

Dog Facts 🐕

◆ Staffordshire Bull Terriers are known for being a robust, versatile, and generally healthy dog breed, but the breed can be prone to hip dysplasia. On average, Staffordshire Bull Terriers can be expected to live between twelve and fourteen years.

◆ In 2019, the Staffordshire Bull Terrier was listed as Britain's most popular dog breed.

◆ A Border Collie named Chaser has learned over a thousand words and has the ability to pair colours with familiar objects and toys to make accurate selections when asked to fetch.

◆ There are over 340 dog breeds, but only around 190 are recognised by the American Kennel Club.

◆ Dogs used to be bred for function, such as herding or guarding. Victorian aristocrats made dog shows and selective breeding fashionable, giving rise to dogs being bred for aesthetic. The Victorians are the reason we enjoy so many different breeds of dog today.

◆ A Neapolitan Mastiff named Tia holds the world record for the largest litter. In November 2004, she gave birth to a litter of twenty-four puppies.

BUDDY

Shereena anxiously tapped her chipped fingernails on the dining room table as she glanced at the clock on the wall. It was 11:30 p.m. on a Thursday and her fiancé, Chris, should have been home hours ago. He was supposed to come straight home after work to take over the care of their three-year-old daughter, Aila. This routine would normally leave Shereena free to head out to her night job, but instead she had waited for hours for Chris to arrive home. Eventually, she had to reluctantly call her manager and inform him that she wouldn't be able to make it to work that night for her shift. She felt hideously guilty as she fibbed down the phone, explaining that her daughter had developed a fever and that if it got much worse she would have to take her to the hospital. Her manager had been understanding of her fabricated crisis, but Shereena still hated lying or letting anyone down.

The UK was experiencing its hottest July on record, and, despite running swivel fans in every room of the house, the heat was still brutal, even at night. Shereena huffed uncomfortably as she felt a bead of sweat run down her neck and soak into her tank top.

Every possible scenario to explain Chris's absence raced
through her mind as she tucked Aila into bed and kissed
her goodnight. Had he been hurt in an accident? Perhaps he
had a family emergency and was so preoccupied with worry
that he didn't think to call home or check his phone for her
voicemails and worried text messages.

The delicious roast chicken which she had meticulously
prepared that evening was now sitting on the dining table,
cold and untouched in a foil tray covered with cling-film.

On the table, she had set
out their best dinner
plates and silverware,
hoping for a quick,
somewhat romantic
dinner before she'd have
to set off for work.
Shereena and Chris had
both been so busy with
their respective jobs that
they rarely had time to
enjoy a meal together. Dinner plans had become brief
back-and-forth text messages about which frozen dinners to
buy, and the longest interactions they had with one another
were only to relieve each other of parenting duties so that
one of them could make it to work on time.

Shereena checked her phone again to see if Chris had replied to her worried messages; nothing.

Shereena extended her arms up above her head and twisted her back slightly. Her elbows and the middle of her spine both clicked as she stretched. From the corner of the room came a muffled grumbling sound. Buddy, a young Pineapple Green Cheeked Conure eyed Shereena in a suspicious fashion, the way a cat might peer from behind a curtain at strangers in their home.

Despite being a small species of parrot, Buddy was remarkably beautiful. From her pale peach-coloured beak to the tip of her red tail feathers, she was scarcely larger than a banana and weighed about as much as a rose. The feathers on her head were also peach in colour, and her wings were a beautiful shade of jungle green. Her orange heart-shaped breast was the most vibrant part of her body, outlined in bright yellow. The yellow feathers extended down Buddy's legs, giving her the appearance of wearing neon-yellow pantaloons, one of Shereena's favourite features on Buddy.

Buddy had only been in Shereena's life for a few short weeks, but, already, it was clear that she was not going to be staying for long in the house. Shereena had lost track of how many times Buddy had bitten her fingers through the bars or escaped from her cage and caused some destruction.

Shereena's mother, Lenise, had presented Buddy to Shereena as a gift at her twenty-ninth birthday celebration earlier that summer in the hopes that she would be good company for her on the days that Chris worked extra-long hours.

Chris, who wasn't much of an animal fan, had not hidden his dislike for Buddy, and Buddy in turn had an aversion to Chris. Whenever he would cross in front of the enclosure to sit on the couch, Buddy would lunge at him and try to bite him through the bars. Their mutual disgust for one another further soured one afternoon when Chris had reached for the TV remote which he had left face-down on top of Buddy's cage, only to find that all of the rubber buttons had been chewed off.

Although Shereena loved animals, she hadn't been seeking a feathery companion, and certainly not such an intelligent species of bird which could inflict such a painful bite. Between her daytime work as a virtual assistant, her night job several times per week as a bartender, and being a full-time mother to a bright and energetic three-year-old child, Shereena felt that she had enough on her plate already. However, her mother had given Buddy to her with good intentions, so Shereena was planning to keep the little parrot a while longer before finding her a new home.

The familiar jangling of Chris's keys caught Shereena's attention, followed by the turning of the brass deadlock on the door. Shereena listened intently as the floorboards creaked under Chris's weight, followed by the usual sound of his toolbox being placed on the floor. Her heart fluttered with relief as she rushed toward the entrance hall to greet her fiancé.

Shereena still felt butterflies in her stomach every time Chris came home. He was tall and fair haired with broad shoulders and just the right amount of stubble which made him look rugged, but not unkempt. His work as a construction supervisor meant that he was often a little dishevelled in a way which she felt was masculine, flattering, and appealing.

"Are you okay?" she asked breathlessly. "I was so worried; I thought you had been in an accident," she added as she instinctively scanned Chris's face and tall frame for any sign of trauma.

"Everything's fine. I just had a long day. Sorry, I really have to sleep," replied Chris as he walked past Shereena, tossed his orange, reflective jacket onto one of the dinner table chairs, pulled off his boots, and, without looking at her or acknowledging the dinner she had lovingly cooked for him, retreated into the darkness of their bedroom.

Through the door, Shereena could see Chris hastily removing the rest of his work clothes. The bedside light illuminated his muscular back as he pulled off his stained vest and tossed it into the laundry hamper on the other side of the bedroom. In an instant, he had climbed into their bed and disappeared under the shiny satin bedsheets which perfectly matched the purple walls.

Shereena was glued to the spot in disbelief. All evening, she had been so worried that a catastrophic emergency had been preventing Chris from coming home. She was completely stunned and confused.

Wary that Chris was acting unusually grouchy, Shereena timidly followed after him into the bedroom where he was lying in bed and facing away from her. She crossed her arms and curled her toes underneath herself swaying slightly on the spot, waiting for the courage to speak.

"I just... I thought you were coming home to take care of Aila because it's Thursday. You never called back, so I had to cancel my work shift," murmured Shereena softly.

"Can we not do this right now?" groaned Chris as he turned his pillow over to enjoy its cooler side. "I really don't need to come home to an interrogation. Just, let me sleep, please."

The cold, harsh tone of his voice made Shereena forget all about the uncomfortable heat wave which had been plaguing the city.

From the bed, Chris could sense Shereena holding her breath. He dreaded the emotional outburst which typically followed when she became anxious or upset. He reached over to the bedside table light and flicked it off, making it clear that he wasn't interested in conversing any further with her for the night.

Shereena exhaled and felt a single disappointed tear fall from her eye and splash against the side of her mouth. She told herself to defuse the situation by leaving Chris alone and letting him sleep, but her hurt was beginning to give way to frustration and anger at his selfishness.

"Aren't you going to kiss your daughter goodnight? She was asking for you all evening."

Chris said nothing. He pulled the covers up farther over his head and remained silent.

Shereena bitterly turned away and walked back toward the living room. Buddy, who had been searching the bottom of her cage for any seeds left in their husks quickly flapped back onto her top perch and shuffled to the back of the enclosure, as far away from Shereena as she could get. Shereena sat quietly at the far end of the sofa, aware that Buddy was uncomfortable with her presence. She stared up at Chris's signed football memorabilia on the wall beside the TV. He could be grumpy at times, but his treatment of her tonight was completely unfair and uncalled for.

Shereena and Chris had experienced their ups and downs, especially following Aila's birth. Chris had struggled to bond with the new baby and felt like a failure for it. No matter how tender or loving he tried to be with Aila, she wouldn't settle in his arms or look at him without bawling loudly. Shereena, who had been overjoyed at the prospect of having a baby girl with the love of her life, and who relished every moment of being pregnant, found herself unexpectedly depressed after the birth. For three long months following Aila's arrival, Shereena felt as though she were trapped in an ever-present darkness which sapped her energy as well as the joy out of being a new mother. Although she knew that postpartum depression was a very common issue and not something to be ashamed of, Shereena had been absolutely certain sure that she wouldn't be affected by it, and, by the time she realised that she was struggling, she felt so much like a maternal failure that she didn't dare confess her secret to anyone. Not even her doctor. Instead, she had relied heavily on Chris to be her emotional crutch.

With time, family life had evolved for Chris and Shereena, and although the fog of postpartum depression did finally lift, new challenges constantly arose, and Shereena often felt as though she was fighting an exhausting, never-ending battle just to get through each day.

Shereena peered across the room and into the kitchen where Aila's colourful artwork was stuck to the refrigerator. Regardless of how hurtful the situation was now, she truly believed that one day in the not-too-distant future, they would find their rhythm as a family together. She just had to continue to be patient.

A low buzzing sound disturbed Shereena's thoughts. She peeled her eyes away from the artwork and glanced at the wood dining table. Thinking that perhaps Tara, her older sister, was calling her for one of their late-night chats, she stood up, passed back in front of Buddy's cage and lifted her phone off the dining table. Her phone screen was blank, but the buzzing continued from deep within Chris's jacket. Shereena hesitated for a moment before her curiosity got the better of her. She slipped her hand into Chris's jacket pocket and retrieved his phone just as the caller gave up. Shereena scanned the home screen of Chris's phone. She could see that her messages to Chris were still suspended in their notification boxes, unopened and ignored. There was an array of other notifications behind her missed calls, but she couldn't view the names of the senders. Looking down the hallway into the dark bedroom, she could see that Chris hadn't stirred. With a pang of guilt, she snuck into the kitchen with the phone and unlocked it. Although she wasn't proud to admit it, she had seen him enter the code into his phone numerous times and had memorized the digits.

Shereena felt her heart begin to race as she tapped on the green chat box icon and opened his text messages. The topmost contact sending him messages was "Dave from Work" who had sent an attachment. Beneath that contact was an unsaved number which looked to be the confirmation notification of a pizza delivery from earlier that evening, and beneath that were Shereena's messages. Shereena's lips curled inwards, irritated that she had spent time and energy on creating a special dinner for Chris to enjoy, when ultimately he had ended up ordering a pizza. Shereena tapped on the contact "Dave from Work," curious as to what sort of image sharing and workplace chatter happened between his workplace buddies.

As the chat box opened, Shereena felt a chill spread throughout her body. This "colleague" had sent Chris a slew of flirtatious messages. The most recent message had been sent less than an hour ago and was a photo of a slender, manicured hand holding up a sock with one finger. The caption read "You left your sock behind. You should come back right now and get it," followed by several lines of heart and winking emojis.

Shereena felt as though the floor had just given way beneath her. Perhaps she was jumping to negative conclusions and there was a rational explanation for these messages? Shereena inhaled through her nostrils and exhaled slowly through her mouth to calm herself down. The messaging app was still open, and her thumb hovered over the contact's telephone number. Without any real plan in place, she called "Dave from Work." Glancing over her shoulder to ensure that Chris was still in bed, she lifted the phone to her ear.

The phone scarcely had time to ring once, when a sultry, deep voice of a woman answered the call.

"I was just thinking about you."

Shereena felt her stomach lurch involuntarily. She covered her mouth and held her breath.

"Chris? Babe?"

Shereena abruptly ended the call and ran toward the bathroom where she lifted the toilet lid and was instantly sick. As she stared into the bowl at the contents of her stomach, she felt hot, angry tears begin to stream down her face. She recognised the purring voice on the other end

of the phone. It was, without a doubt, her friend Chelsea.
Shereena and Chelsea had worked together for several
years as brand ambassadors, selling VIP passes and cocktail
vouchers for high-end clubs. Their contrasting beauty had
made their teamwork wildly successful. Chelsea was a tall and
voluptuous blonde from Wales, with devastating blue eyes
and an hourglass figure which never failed to turn heads. In
contrast, Shereena was an exotic beauty of mixed British and
Mauritian heritage, with mocha skin, a petite frame, pixie-like
features, and warming almond eyes. Together, they would
routinely outsell and outperform every other sales team.
Sharing a mutual love for club life and music festivals, they
had become close friends over the years, though they had
seen much less of each other since Aila was born.

Shereena stood up, flushed, and reached for the bottle of
bleach behind the toilet. She squirted some of the solution
into the bowl, the smell of the bleach making her feel even
more nauseous. Still holding Chris's phone in one hand, she
furiously shovelled water from the sink faucet into her mouth
and rinsed over and over. Her mind was somersaulting
between anger and disbelief. As she wiped her mouth dry
with a towel, she heard the low, grunting sound of Chris's
snoring coming from the bedroom. How could he possibly
come home and sleep so soundly in their bed while hiding
an infidelity?

Shereena paced back and forth in the bathroom. She knew that the best course of action would be to try to get some rest and then confront Chris calmly over the weekend. Out of the corner of her eye, Shereena caught sight of one of Chris's socks lying discarded by the bathtub. As she bent down to pick up the forgotten garment, all she could see in her mind was the photo that Chelsea had sent to Chris. Shereena picked up the sock and angrily tossed it out of the open window above the toilet. She whipped around, wiped her tears dry and began to walk up the hallway to the bedroom, passing Aila's along the way. From inside the small, pink bedroom she could hear the sound machine playing seaside noises which helped Aila to sleep at night. She clenched Chris's phone tightly in her clammy hand as she continued to march up the hallway and into the master bedroom. There, on his back, one leg out of the bed and an arm flopped over his face was Chris, sleeping soundly without a single care for how badly his actions were hurting his fiancée. For a moment, Shereena almost considered throwing the phone in her hand straight at Chris's cheating head.

Shereena steadied herself against the bedroom doorframe as she slowly extended her arm around the door, felt for the light switch and flicked it on.

Like a vampire confronted with a sunrise, Chris immediately began to contort and writhe. He groaned and pulled the purple bedcovers up over his head. From the darkness of the duvet, he mumbled for Shereena to switch off the light. Shereena couldn't hold her tongue in any longer.

"How long have you been cheating on me?" she asked. She was quietly impressed with how firm she was able to sound. Under the bed covers, Chris went completely rigid. After what seemed like an age, he slowly sat up and for the first time since he had arrived home that night, looked into Shereena's eyes.

"That's crazy, baby. I don't even know what you're saying right now," he said, wearing his most sincere expression.

His blatant lies disarmed and unravelled Shereena in an instant.

She began to sob involuntarily and doubled over, her hand covering her mouth. Leaning against the door frame, she slid down to the floor.

"You liar!" she shouted, hurling the phone across the room where it hit the headboard and landed next to Chris.

"Jesus!" he exclaimed as he snatched up his phone and inspected it for any damage. "You've been spying on me?" he hissed at her.

Shereena picked herself up off the floor and walked around the bed until she towered over Chris. "Don't you dare turn this around on me. You cheated on me. I trusted you, and you cheated on me. Why would you do this to us?"

Chris said nothing. His eyes were fixed on the foot of the bed where he was moving his toes around under the sheets. His expression was irritatingly remorseless.

"Why, Chris? We have a daughter! We're getting married."

"We're not getting married, Shereena," Chris murmured, cutting her off.

Shereena felt another pang of pain stab at her core. His expression was one of quiet defeat. He sighed and crossed his arms across his bare chest as he rested his head against the headboard and peered up at her.

"Chelsea and I... We're not just messing around. We're in love. We've been in love for a while, and we were waiting for the right time to tell you."

Shereena was suddenly aware of how hot and stuffy the room felt. Her mouth seemed to instantly dry and her stomach dropped in the way that it did on the dip of a rollercoaster ride. Inside, she was screaming, but she couldn't muster a single sound.

Chris sighed and pulled himself to the opposite side of the bed where he stood up and walked out of the bedroom. Shereena was stunned and felt as though she was looking in on someone else's life. Nothing felt real.

The sound of shuffling and small noises coming from the bathroom brought Shereena back from her faraway state.

Gathering up her courage, she peered down the hallway. She could see Chris gathering up his toiletries and throwing them into his wash kit.

"What are you doing?" asked Shereena weakly she approached him.

"I can't stay here," said Chris. "I can't deal with the betrayal of you spying on me."

Chris's tone was matter of fact and detached. He clearly meant what he was saying, and Shereena felt herself begin to panic and spiral. Her life was unravelling at an overwhelming pace.

"What about us? What about Aila?" she appealed quietly to him, hoping that he would come to his senses. Her heart was beating painfully fast.

He scooped up his wash kit and made his way quickly back to the bedroom, walking straight past Shereena. He shook open one of his backpacks and began roughly stuffing clothes inside it. Shereena stared on in disbelief as he reached past their family photo on his bedside table and yanked his phone charger out of the electrical socket. Zipping up his backpack, he scanned the room one last time before making his way out through the bedroom door and into the living room.

"Can't we figure this out? Please don't leave me," Shereena pleaded.

Chris began to shimmy his feet into his work boots and put his jacket on. He didn't respond or give any indication that he was listening.

"Please, Chris, I love you!" she cried. Her entire body was trembling as she slipped in front of Chris and hugged him tightly around his middle.

Chris recoiled, repulsed at Shereena's unwanted touch. He clasped his huge hands around her tiny forearms and peeled himself free of her desperate grasp.

"Touch me again and you'll see what happens," growled Chris as he used his far larger frame to shove Shereena out of the way. As he pushed past her, he accidentally sent her dainty body crashing into a side table. The whole table shook from the force of Shereena's impact, and the decorative lamp which sat upon it toppled over and smashed on the floor at her feet.

Chris paused and looked down at Shereena, crumpled on the floor. Littered around her were broken shards of coloured glass.

"Are you hurt?" he asked coldly. Dazed, Shereena shook her head. Without another word, Chris turned away once again and continued toward the door.

Shereena felt suspended and detached from her body, like a puppet controlled by someone else pulling her strings. Pieces of glass crunched and clinked under her Converse shoes as she stood up. Shereena turned to the closest thing she could hold—the roast chicken she had made for their dinner. Her mind went blank as she picked it up and hurled it with all her might at Chris. Time seemed to stand still as the tray flew through the air and made contact with his back. The juices and gravy which had collected over several hours in the foil tray splashed across his neon orange jacket, instantly leaving deep grease stains.

The chicken fell heavily to the floor with a thud, followed by the metallic clang of the tray. Buddy, who had been quietly watching the exchange, was startled and let out a piercing squawk.

Shereena immediately regretted her impulsive action and began to apologise over and over in a high-pitched voice, skipping toward Chris. He furiously whipped around and glared at Shereena. His face was flushed red and his mouth was twisted into a scowl. Having reached his limit, he spoke in a low and threatening voice.

"This is why I can't be near you. I'm sick of your craziness, Shereena. I'm not a doctor and you need help." His light blue eyes flared at her with unfiltered hatred. "I'll get the rest of my stuff when I'm ready. Don't call me."

With one final look of pure disgust, Chris turned his back on Shereena and stormed out of the door into the humid night, leaving a shiny trail of gravy and grease behind him.

Shereena was rooted to the spot, trying to make sense of everything that had just happened. Still completely dazed, she reached for the front door, which was wide open, swaying gently on its hinges. She looked out into the night and saw Chris hastily power walking up the quiet residential street, the reflective stripes on his jacket shimmering under the streetlights.

Shereena closed the front door and turned to look at the mess in the living room. The roast chicken was lying beaten on the ground. Its brown, crispy skin had sloughed off and was congealing on the floor among the shards of broken glass.

"Mummy?" came a little voice from across the room. Aila had woken up and was standing at the edge of the hallway, rubbing her sleepy eyes. Her caramel hair was messy from where she had been lying on it, and, in her hand, she clutched her pink and white security blanket.

Shereena gasped and hopped over the mangled mess in the living room. She crouched down to embrace her daughter.

"Why are you out of bed, Lala?"

Aila melted into her mother's embrace.

"Is daddy home?" she asked in her sweet little voice.

Shereena bit her lip as she hugged her tightly. She had to reach deep into her core to find the strength to hold back her tears.

"Daddy's not home yet," she said in the most normal tone that she could muster.

"Why is the chicken on the floor?" asked Aila, peering through her mother's dark hair.

Shereena straightened up and hoisted her tiny daughter up onto her hip.

"Well," she said. "The chicken tried to fly away. He made a very big mess, didn't he? What a naughty chicken!" she said, carrying Aila back to her bedroom, feeling grateful that Aila had not witnessed the messy altercation just moments before.

Once Shereena was certain that Aila was settled back into bed and Shereena reset the sound machine, she returned to the living room and began to clean up the mess. She replayed the night's dramatic events over and over in her head as she carefully swept up the glass, peeled the spent chicken off of the floor, and mopped up the mangled remnants of skin and gravy.

Shereena forced herself into bed at three o'clock where she began to cry once more, softly at first and then harder until she found herself wailing and unable to catch her breath. She loathed Chris for cheating on her, but the bed felt so alien and empty without him. She reached out over to his side of the bed in the darkness, somehow hoping that she would feel his warm body beside her, but knowing full well she was reaching out to nothing. She pulled his pillow over to herself and hugged it tightly. She could still smell his light, earthy scent on it. The smell did little to comfort her as she wrapped the covers around herself and tried to imagine that she was in nestled safely in Chris's arms, the way they used to fall asleep together years ago when life was easier, carefree, and their arguments were trivial and held no consequences.

Through the open window, Shereena could hear the faint sound of a blackbird singing in the distance. She clenched her eyes shut and buried her face deeper into Chris's pillow. She prayed that if any benevolent force might be witnessing her pain that it would somehow make things right again and bring the man she loved back to her.

Shereena was startled from her sleep by the shrill sound of the house telephone. She tried to open her eyes, but they were swollen and covered in crust. Still mostly asleep, Shereena stumbled out of bed and into the living room toward the telephone.

"Hello?" she croaked as she picked up the receiver.

"Hi, Shereena, it's Susan calling from Bunny Hops Nursery. We were just wondering if Aila would be coming in today."

Shereena threw her head over her shoulder to the clock on the wall. It was almost ten o'clock. She should have dropped off Aila at preschool two hours ago, and she should already be replying to emails for her online clients.

She screwed her face up and gripped the phone receiver hard as she recalled the events of the previous night. She whipped around and scanned the living room, entrance hall, and kitchen for her daughter, but couldn't see her.

"I'm afraid Aila has a bit of a sore throat this morning. I'm going to keep her home for the day. So sorry I forgot to call— we'll see you on Monday!" Shereena hung up the receiver before the nursery receptionist could reply.

She bolted toward Aila's bedroom, praying that she hadn't wandered off.

As she tumbled into Aila's room, she found her daughter sprawled on her bed, surrounded by every cuddly toy in her bedroom.

"Mummy, I have to potty now," she said as she squirmed uncomfortably.

Shereena picked up Aila from the bed and quickly shuttled her into the bathroom. Worse than fighting with Chris and having him walk out on her was the feeling that in her grief-stricken state, she was letting Aila down. It was a huge wakeup call for Shereena, who felt like the worst parent in the world.

Shereena settled her relieved daughter down on the sofa with a bowl of sliced banana and her favourite Disney

DVD. Buddy, whose enclosure was next to the couch, began chirping loudly, making it known that she too would like some breakfast. Shereena groaned as she realised that with all that had happened the previous night, she had completely forgotten to feed Buddy her evening meal. She scooped a small slice of banana from Aila's bowl and pushed it through the bars of the cage. The little bird's inky black eyes lit up with delight as she gratefully nibbled the banana and methodically rolled the deliciously mushy fruit all over her tongue.

Reaching under the large white cage, Shereena grabbed a tin containing a custom mix of specially-formulated Conure pellets, seeds, nuts, and dried fruit. Buddy began to chirp and bob her head excitedly in anticipation of her tasty banquet. Shereena tipped a generous amount of the mix into Buddy's food cup and placed it back into its holder within the cage.

Buddy waited until Shereena had stepped back from the cage a few paces before she felt safe enough to fly down to the feeding station. Methodically, Buddy began sorting through the seed mixture to find the food items she prized the most. Shereena sighed as Buddy expertly used her tough beak to push and spray the mixture in every direction, sending many of the seeds onto the living room floor. When she finally uncovered a slice of freeze-dried banana, she picked up the fruit and purposefully carried it over to her water bowl where she promptly plopped it into the water. Initially, Shereena had been frustrated whenever Buddy did this with the dried bananas, because it would inevitably cloud and foul up the water, but she soon came to realise that this was Buddy's way of softening the tougher pieces of dried fruit. She was using water as a tool to make her dinner times more enjoyable!

Shereena smiled as Buddy gripped the soggy piece of fruit in one of her feet and quickly nibbled away at it. She pulled out her phone, eager to take a picture of Buddy eating, but the sight of the phone caused the bird to flap in alarm, abandon her food, and fly back up to the perch which was furthest away from Shereena. She sighed and crossed in front of the television where Aila was engrossed in a Disney film. She slid open the patio door. She stepped barefoot out onto the tiled patio and immediately felt the sun's warming rays on her skin. Shereena peered at her phone. She had several email requests from her clients, but no messages or calls from Chris.

Not fully clear on her motives, Shereena opened her Facebook app and searched for Chris. She was confused to find that she couldn't locate him anywhere on the app. She then checked on Instagram and then Twitter—nothing. She had been completely blocked on all of his social media platforms.

Frustrated, Shereena searched for Chelsea's Facebook page. Chelsea had deleted Shereena off of Facebook, but her posts were still visible to the public. Shereena scrolled through the sea of selfies captioned with motivational quotes. Although she wanted to reach out and tell Chelsea what she thought of her, she instead chose to close the app and go back inside to tend to her daughter, determined to hold herself together.

Shereena stepped back inside the house and settled onto the couch for a moment with Aila, who was happily shuffling in her seat and watching her film. Frightening questions began to race through Shereena's mind. How would she manage to pay the bills alone? How would she juggle her work schedule without Chris? Shereena thankfully had some small savings. It wasn't much, but it could, if managed sensibly, at least afford her a few weeks to pick herself up and reorganise her life.

Aila snuggled into her mother, who placed a loving kiss on her head. Shereena inhaled the sweet scent of her baby girl. It was her favourite smell in the world and never failed to make her troubles melt away for a few moments at a time.

For all of their relationship problems and struggles over the years, Shereena had truly believed that both she and Chris would stand the test of time, if only to provide Aila with a stable and loving home.

As the day dragged on painfully and Shereena tried her best to handle her work emails, she kept finding herself longing for Chris. She couldn't understand how she had not noticed that he had been drifting so far away from her. They had both been busy with their work schedules, but Shereena hadn't expected Chris use their conflicting schedules as an opportunity to pursue other women. In what precious little time they were able to spend together, Shereena had always tried her best to create a happy and healthy family environment. She had been learning to cook more protein-rich dishes for Chris, who had developed a keen interest in fitness and health. She had given up her usual pampering time where she would paint her nails spectacular colours to instead spend more time cleaning the house and creating a more enjoyable space. She had invested all of her heart and effort into their family life, only to be discarded.

That evening, after dinner, Shereena was settling Aila into her pyjamas when the inevitable question which she had been dreading squeaked out of her daughter's mouth.

"Where is daddy?"

Shereena hesitated as she buttoned up Aila's koala bear onesie. In truth, a small part of her believed that Chris would have realised by now how much he loved his family and returned home to them.

"Daddy has to work very, very far away, Lala," she said softly as she fastened the last button.

"Ooh," said Aila, as though she had a great understanding of her father's job.

"Is Nana coming soon?" she added brightly, squashing two of her stuffed animal toys together in an embrace.

Shereena's heart filled with love for her sweet little girl. It was so unfair that she had to be without her father, and for such selfish reasons. At the very least, Shereena had hoped that Chris would have wanted to make arrangements to see his daughter at the weekend, but he still hadn't called or replied to her messages earlier that day. His abandonment of such a happy and loving child was not something she could ever understand.

"Yes, Lala. Nana is coming to see you tomorrow."

At two in the morning, Shereena found herself once again sitting woefully in her dark bedroom. The curtains were drawn tightly shut, but still a small sliver of light was creeping into her bedroom, illuminating Chris's shoe collection.

Shereena clutched at one of Chris's hoodies as tears escaped from her eyes and ran down her flushed cheeks. She hated herself and her inability to handle the trauma she was feeling. Perhaps Chris was right. Maybe she was crazy. Who would want to stay with a crazy person?

The weekend provided Shereena with a welcome break from her loneliness as her mother, Lenise, stopped by to visit her and Aila. Despite feeling so low, Shereena managed to put on a brave face and pretend that nothing was wrong. When her mother had asked where Chris was, Shereena had pretended that he was away on a lads' weekend with some old friends from school. She couldn't bear to reveal the truth, in part because she didn't want her mother to worry about her, but mostly because Shereena didn't want to turn her family against Chris, not if there was a chance that they might still reconcile.

Shereena adored having her mother over on the weekends. Aila was completely besotted with her Nana and rarely had eyes for anyone else whenever she visited, perhaps because she was always the most colourfully dressed in a room. Today was no exception—Lenise wore a white, floor length skirt, a pink T-shirt, and an assortment of aquamarine, white, and pink silk flowers clipped in her hair. Physically speaking, Lenise was the complete opposite of her daughter. Her hair was blond and shoulder length, and she had porcelain skin which was a stark contrast to her children, who all had the same exotic skin that Shereena had.

Shereena smiled as she watched her daughter and mother
draw colourful pictures on the floor with crayons. She hadn't
always been so close to her mother. In fact, their arguments
during her teenage years could be heard up and down the
River Thames. Shereena often avoided bringing her school
friends home with her for fear of being embarrassed by
her eccentric mother. Each year, Shereena would cringe as
Lenise would create her over-the-top Christmas displays,
which would go up in November and stay up all the way
until the spring. Lenise had collected immaculate taxidermy
woodland creatures, such as rabbits, European badgers, a fox,
and a magpie, the latter of which was so well articulated that
it looked ready to peck at anything shiny. Lenise would put up
a huge Christmas tree in the living room and painstakingly
hand-spray it with thick layers of fake snow, and beneath the
tree, nestled in even more fake snow, she would position the
taxidermy animals in a way which made the scene feel alive.

In recent years, Shereena had found a deep appreciation for
her mother's wisdom, her love for all living creatures, and
her unique interests, including the collection of rare orchids
and vacuum cleaners.

Aila had finished colouring her latest masterpiece, a brown
rainbow. She waved it like a flag in front of Shereena's face,
evidently proud of her creation. Shereena scooped it up and
animatedly cooed over and applauded its earthy tones. She

crossed the living room into the kitchen and secured the drawing to the front of the refrigerator with a magnet.

"Shall we see if Buddy wants to play?" asked Lenise to Aila.

"Yay!" squealed Aila in reply, taking her grandmother's hand and pulling her over to Buddy's cage.

Shereena watched nervously from the kitchen as her mother casually opened Buddy's enclosure and pressed her index finger lightly against the temperamental bird's orange breast. Buddy opened her beak into a threatening gape, ready to defend herself.

"Step up," said Lenise brightly as she gently pushed her finger farther into Buddy's breast, and in one motion, pulled her hand upwards, causing Buddy to have to step up onto her finger.

"What a good bird!" she praised. Buddy tilted her head to the side and stared intently at Lenise. Shereena watched in amazement as her mother lifted Buddy out of the enclosure and into the living room without any bloodshed.

"Careful, mum, she bites!" warned Shereena, stepping closer to her mother in case an intervention was needed. Lenise raised the vibrant bird up to her eye level and began making soft kissing sounds.

"Of course she bites!" she replied. "She's a scared baby bird who is trying to communicate with you in the only way she knows how."

Buddy, who was normally either completely rigid at the slightest touch, or ready to lunge and bite, began chirping and making peculiar gurgling noises while bobbing her head up and down animatedly.

Lenise nodded her head up and down, mimicking Buddy and began verbally praising the parrot with short expressions such as "Yes!," "Good bird!" and "Who's a show-off!?"

Aila waddled over to the sofa next to Buddy's enclosure and clumsily climbed up onto its thick cushions to get a better view of the exciting things her grandmother was doing with Buddy.

"Parrots are perpetual three-year-olds," continued Lenise to Shereena. "You'll get the best from her if you take the time to learn who she is, what she enjoys, and what frightens her. Show her that you're an intelligent creature who is capable of learning and listening."

Lenise reached into the pocket of her flowing skirt and pulled out small pieces of shaved almond.

"Find out what her favourite snacks are, and only feed them to her when she comes out to interact with you," said Lenise as she lifted an almond piece up to Buddy's face. "Where diplomacy fails, food prevails!"

Buddy immediately snatched up the morsel of shaved almond and quickly transferred it to her left foot, which she used much like a hand. Gripping the almond tightly, Buddy nibbled at it with gusto, and in mere moments, the treat had been reduced to only a few powdery crumbs on the back of Lenise's thumb.

Lenise turned to face Shereena and beckoned her to lift up a finger. Buddy, who had been gently feeling Lenise's hand with her beak, hoping to find more almonds, gazed intently at Shereena. Lenise took her daughter's hand in her own and guided her extended index finger upwards to encourage Buddy to step up. To Shereena's delight, Buddy did step up. Her beak opened wide, which almost made Shereena want to pass her back to her mother, but instead she softly spoke to the bird, asking if she wanted a treat. Lenise passed her daughter a piece of shaved almond, which Buddy was quick to recognise as a scrumptious snack and so allowed Shereena to place the treat in her beak. Buddy ate the treat heartily and gave Shereena a small, appreciative chirp. Aila clapped her hands together in applause for her mother. Lenise gave her daughter a warm nod of approval as she witnessed the magic of a new friendship forming before her eyes.

"Can I hold Buddy?" asked Aila from the sofa.

"Let's not overwhelm her," replied Lenise. "We don't want to scare her. When Buddy is more used to coming out with Mummy, then you can hold her, but you have to make sure that Mummy holds Buddy every day, okay? Can you do Nana a favour and remind Mummy to hold Buddy every day, Lala?"

Aila furiously nodded her head, seemingly pleased with her grandmother's instructions, and slipped off of the sofa to run outside and play with her water table.

"Mum, why do you have shaved almonds in your skirt?" asked Shereena.

"Squirrels like them," replied Lenise. "And they're wonderful for healthy hair!" she added, flipping her hair like a shampoo model as she and her daughter chuckled together.

Over the next week, Aila surprised Shereena by insisting that she must keep her promise to Nana. Every morning, Aila would demand that Shereena bring out Buddy for a good morning almond and allow the bird to sit at the table to eat breakfast with them. In fact, Aila refused to eat her own breakfast if Buddy wasn't also eating hers at the table. Buddy

seemed to thoroughly enjoy being allowed to sit at the table
for breakfast, and, in only three days, Buddy had learned that
once Aila was sitting at the table, it signified that Shereena
was about to let Buddy out of her cage and bring her almonds
with breakfast.

Aila squealed with delight as she would flick Cheerio's
into the centre of the table, and Buddy would collect them
up and bring them back to her. For such a small bird,
Buddy had so much character and provided Aila with
endless companionship. It was a very special moment for
them all one night after story time when Shereena lifted
her daughter's hand up and carefully guided Buddy onto
her fingers.

Buddy had provided so
much positive focus for
both Aila and Shereena.
Instead of spending her
lunch hour obsessively
refreshing Chelsea's
Facebook page and
looking for status
updates, Shereena began
reading parrot care blog
posts and watching DIY
videos on YouTube about

how to create safe, mentally stimulating toys for Conures out of household objects.

Buddy, though still shy of some loud noises, began to blossom rapidly into a confident and cheeky bird. Rather than sitting in her enclosure, frozen and statuesque, she began to explore Shereena's homemade toys and vocalize in new and experimental ways. She had also developed the confidence to climb up Shereena's arm and perch on her shoulder. Shereena had begun to allow Buddy to free-roam the living room under supervision during her daytime office hours while Aila was away at nursery. She had needed to get creative in order to parrot-proof the room as best as possible, but the payoff was hugely uplifting; she was able to open Buddy's enclosure so that Buddy could explore at her leisure and seek out company whenever she felt like it.

Weeknights were also beginning to become easier to manage. Shereena had employed a babysitter to care for Aila and Buddy a few evenings per week, leaving her free to go back to her evening job at the bar.

After three weeks of adjusting to a new routine, Shereena was still feeling conflicted. A part of her still dared to hope that Chris would come home and that they would be able to work through their problems for Aila, but another part of her unexpectedly began to enjoy having her own space. She was no longer treading on eggshells around someone who was supposed to be her best friend, and she was beginning to think of new and exciting possibilities her and Aila. Chris had never wanted to go anywhere or explore any place farther away from London than he could comfortably reach on the Underground, so they'd never gone on a real holiday before. Shereena had always loved to travel internationally, and she was warmed by the prospect of being able to take Aila to faraway places where she could experience the world beyond London.

Shereena pondered all of this heavily during her sacred bath time late at night. She often found that she was able to think most clearly when she was relaxing in the bath, and Buddy had begun to make herself a part of this routine, either perching contently on the side of the bathtub or attacking the luffa. On this particular night, Shereena had a moment of clarity where she realised that she had always been the one to make sacrifice after sacrifice in their relationship. She used to love going to music festivals but couldn't remember the last time she went to one. Instead, she had lost count of the number of times she had been persuaded to go with Chris to the pub and watch football, which she hated.

She used to enjoy watching quirky films, like *Labyrinth*, *The Dark Crystal*, and *The Princess Bride*, but she couldn't

remember the last time she watched one when Chris lived
with her because he found the movies "creepy."

Shereena raised her leg in the bathtub and watched the
soapy suds drip slowly down toward the bathtub. How had
she let this happen? When did she make the subconscious
decision that it was okay to slowly chisel away at what
made her unique and happy in order to accommodate
another's comfort?

Buddy's little talons clicked as she marched along the edge
of the bathtub, craning her neck out in order to nip at
the bubbles.

Shereena knew that as painful as it would be, she couldn't
live in the past forever. Chris had still not made any contact,
and Shereena began to doubt if Chris would ever return
home for his belongings. His clothes still hung in the
wardrobe and his beloved collection of overpriced sports
shoes still gave him a presence in the house which distracted
Shereena daily. It was hard to be constantly surrounded by
memories they had made together, such as the bedroom
walls they had randomly decided to paint purple, or the tacky
curtains which Chris had chosen.

Shereena had just entered her bedroom when her mobile
phone began to ring. It was her older sister, Tara. Although

Shereena and Tara were close, they usually arranged to have late-night calls through text message first, so Shereena realised that something was either very wrong or very important to warrant a sudden phone call so late at night.

Accepting the call, Shereena held her phone up to her ear.

"Hello? Shereena?" came Tara's concerned voice over the line.

"Hi Tara, are you okay?" asked Shereena, worried that she was about to be told some devastating news.

"You're asking me if I'm okay? I'm fine! What I want to know is when you were going to tell us about Chris?"

Shereena's mouth fell open and she slowly sat on her bed.

"I don't—what do you mean?" replied Shereena, doing her best not to give anything away.

"Chris just changed his Facebook relationship status. It says he's 'Engaged' to Chelsea Evans, and people are responding like it's real. What happened?"

All at once, the pain which Shereena had believed was beginning to fade came rushing back to her. She couldn't produce a single sound, let alone begin to explain to her sister the hell she had been living through by herself for the past three weeks.

The tiny hope that Shereena had been holding onto for reconciliation had been small and fragile, flickering dimly inside her like the final moments of a candle burning before it runs out of wick. Now, she realised that Chris had made his final decision, and he had done so in the most painfully nonchalant way possible. By announcing his new engagement to the world without even having the decency to break off his engagement to Shereena, he had robbed her of the chance to inform her family of their split, and he had denied Shereena the privacy she would need to come to terms with this huge life change. His willingness to discard Shereena and Aila in such a public manner was a cruelty which Shereena had never thought him capable of.

With immense difficulty, Shereena began to recount to her sister how her relationship had fallen apart. Tara dutifully and sympathetically listened to Shereena as she finally stopped pretending to be okay and allowed her carefully orchestrated facade to crumble. Through the two-hour chat on the bed, Buddy stayed nestled on Shereena's shoulder, nuzzling and nibbling her cheek affectionately with her beak. Once Shereena had finished sharing her grief and her worries, Tara assured her that with the help of family and good friends, she would not only get through this ordeal, but thrive. It was a huge relief for Shereena to hear Tara say that the family never liked Chris much, but tolerated him for her sake. She also offered to break the news on Shereena's behalf to various family members to save Shereena from having to suffer the same questions again and again. Shereena shed one last tear of relief as Tara promised her that Aila would never suffer from any sort of love deficiency.

"It's going to be okay, Shereena" said Tara. "You still have your family, and we're all here for you."

Tara instructed Shereena to keep her phone on and to expect visitors at the weekend.

It was scarcely ten o'clock on Saturday when Shereena's doorbell rang. Buddy chirped and whistled loudly to herald the arrival of guests at the door. Shereena, dressed in overalls, a white T-shirt and her Converse, opened the door to see her mother, Tara, and two of her best friends crowded around her doorstep. Her mother was holding two bags full of new bedding and curtains, and Tara was holding flowers and a small tray of colourful cupcakes.

The sight of her family stirred up a huge tidal wave of love and gratitude in Shereena, and she broke into her first real smile in weeks.

"Nana!" squealed Aila, running toward Lenise and
hugging her legs.

The energy was jubilant as the group of visitors rallied
behind Shereena to help her spring clean the entire house.

Every dark curtain was torn down and sorted into bags, ready
to be donated. Each window was thrown open, allowing the
summer sun to stream into the house from every angle. In the
bedroom, Shereena's friends played the most iconic, cheesy
songs from 1990s as they splashed white paint over the patchy
dark purple walls, and, on the patio, Aila was showing her
grandmother how fast she could spin like a helicopter.

Shereena and Tara tackled the task of bundling Chris's
clothes and shoes into black dustbin bags. Tara had insisted
that since Chris was no longer contributing to the home
and had moved on, Shereena was not obligated to donate
her space and awareness to his belongings. With every bag
of clothes that was bundled up and carried out of the house
to be placed on the pavement, Shereena felt lighter and
liberated. She had to retreat to the bathroom for a quiet
moment to shed tears of relief—the last tears she would
need to cry for a long time to come. Shereena had been
reminded that it's okay to ask for help, and that starting over
didn't have to be as scary as she had worked it up to be in
her mind. After composing herself, she walked out into the

living room and was pleasantly surprised to see how bright and serene the room now looked with new curtains and fresh flowers. The sports-themed art and video games which Chris has insisted on displaying in the room were now gone, and in their place were canvas photo collages of family, friends, and even some recent photos Shereena had managed to take of Buddy.

"I just guessed which photos you'd like best," came Tara's voice from the kitchen. Shereena turned around and hugged her sister tightly.

"It's wonderful. Thank you."

As Tara squeezed her little sister back, a thought ran through her mind.

"Hey, Shereena, can I ask you a question? Did you really throw a chicken at Chris?"

Shereena looked up at her sister guiltily, and they both burst out in laughter.

Within hours, the house looked and felt completely different. Hanging above the newly cleaned patio doors were delicate, sheer white curtains with intricate shimmery gold leaf patterns. The bedroom walls were now white, and the bed was hugged by soft, oatmeal-coloured sheets.

Outside on the pavement were seven bags full of Chris's belongings, shimmering against the pink and orange sunset. Shereena snapped a photo of the pile and sent it Chris with the simple message: "The rest of your stuff. Don't call me."

Sending Chris that text message felt like a huge victory for Shereena. Throughout their relationship, she had always walked on eggshells, fearful that she might do or say something wrong, and desperately afraid that Chris would leave her, forcing her to navigate life alone.

Knowing that she had faced and survived her worst fear was profoundly liberating. Shereena looked down at her phone and smiled secretly to herself as she swiped her finger across the screen to decline Chris's first phone call to her since he had walked out. What Chris wanted to say, she didn't care to know. Her space was now completely cleansed of his narcissism, lies, and control and she would never again afford any person that power over herself.

As night fell, Shereena's friends reminded her that she was not alone when they hugged her goodbye and departed into the warm night.

Lenise and Tara stayed behind a little while longer, allowing Shereena the chance to talk some more if she felt she needed to. As Tara played with her niece, Lenise observed Buddy in her cage.

"How are you getting along with Buddy? I understand if she's too much for you to handle right now."

Shereena smiled at her mother and walked toward Buddy's enclosure. She lifted the metal catch on the cage door, opened it, and took several steps back. Lenise beamed with pride as Shereena whistled a short tune to Buddy, who flew straight over to her finger and perched on it proudly, waiting for a treat. From her pocket, Shereena pulled out a small piece of shaved almond and held it up so that Lenise could see it. Neither Shereena nor her mother could contain their laughter. Tara stared over at her mother and sister from where she was sat with Aila. She was completely lost as to why anyone would keep shaved almonds in their pockets.

Alone, though far from lonely, Shereena sank back into the plush new pillows on her bed and enjoyed the smell of her brand new sheets. Aila had fallen asleep under her arm during their evening story time, and Buddy was nestled in Aila's lap, her eyelids drooping as she battled to stay awake. Shereena reached over with her free arm and gently scratched Buddy on the side of her cheek. Her feathers fluffed upwards in contentment.

As she delicately placed Buddy back onto her favourite sleeping perch in her enclosure, Shereena felt a sense of finally being at home with herself. It had taken her twenty-

nine years, many mistakes, and several hurtful betrayals for her to realise that she—and she alone—held the key to her own happiness. She no longer felt any shame that she had placed her faith in the wrong person, and although she still hoped for a kind and loving father figure for Aila in the future, Shereena had no doubt that Aila would be raised with the help of the most loving tribe of friends and family. That night, for the first time, the house truly felt like a home. For Shereena, happiness didn't come in the form of a happy ending. It came in the form of a new beginning, a new world of possibilities for her beloved Lala, and a tiny bird with a huge personality.

Parrot Facts 🦜

- Conures are "New World" birds, meaning that they are found in the Western hemisphere. All living Conure species live in Central and South America.

- Conures are typically more social than their larger parrot cousins such as cockatoos. They are known for being social with multiple family members, instead of bonding closely to one person and shunning others.

- Pineapple Green Cheeked Conures have lifespans of up to thirty years.

- Conures are often referred to as the clowns of the parrot world for their attention-seeking antics, such as dancing, stomping their feet as they walk, and hanging upside down.

- The oldest documented parrot ever to have lived was Cookie, a Major Mitchell's cockatoo. She was at least eighty-two years and eighty-eight days old. Some other parrot keepers and zoos claim to have the oldest living parrots, but so far, Cookie is the only parrot with credible evidence to back up her claim.

- African Grey parrots are famed for being the best talkers. Their ability to learn and mimic sounds is unrivalled by other parrots, however, the master of all mimicry is actually a bird which is not a parrot at all. The Superb Lyrebird, a ground-dwelling bird from Australia, is famed for its elaborate repertoire of calls. Lyrebirds can mimic around forty different species of birds in a single mating call. They don't only mimic other Australian birds, such as Kookaburras, they can also mimic human-made sounds such as chainsaws, cell phones, and camera shutters.

BUBBLES

Ragnar squinted through his sunglasses and swerved his black pickup truck over onto the emergency stopping lane of the freeway.

Leaving his engine running and his blinkers on, he jogged along the dusty shoulder, careful not to step on the pieces of shredded rubber and broken glass which littered the edge of the tarmac.

Scarcely an hour before, a concerned school bus driver had driven past the stretch of road and spotted a pile of discarded animal cages. Fearing that there might be abandoned kittens or puppies in the carriers, the driver had contacted a local animal rescue which had dispatched Ragnar, one of their wildlife rehabbers and a seasoned rescuer, to investigate the site.

Ragnar did not look like a typical rescuer or someone who had a huge soft spot for animals. In fact, he looked more like a Viking who had travelled through time and space and somehow ended up in Detroit. His waist-length, strawberry-blonde hair was pulled back into a bun, and his long red and blonde beard was plaited in several places.

Ragnar slowed his jog down to a walking pace as he
approached the carelessly dumped pet supplies. In a messy
pile were cracked and shattered aquariums of assorted sizes,
filthy old pet carriers, and bundles of tangled electrical wires.
Ragnar slipped his hand into his jacket pocket and pulled
out his phone to document the deserted goods. Although
he knew it was unlikely that the culprit would ever be found
(and, if they were, would likely never be brought to justice for
littering) gathering evidence was standard protocol.

Ragnar reached into the back pocket of his jeans and pulled
out a pair of heavy-duty gloves. He had often worn these
when handling large injured wildlife like deer, but their
density also offered ideal protection when he had to search
through piles of unknown waste.

Careful not cut himself on the jagged aquarium glass, Ragnar
searched meticulously through each tank, scouring for any
signs of life. He then moved over to the cracked pet carriers.
They were cheap, poorly made carriers in garish colours, but,
thankfully, each carrier was empty save for ancient rabbit
droppings and old hay which smelled faintly of ammonia
and mildew.

Concerned that there might be an abandoned rabbit
somewhere along the stretch of road, Ragnar cautiously
walked a few yards up the shoulder of the freeway. He passed

the mummified remains of a raccoon and some old pigeon feathers, but he couldn't find any rabbits.

Glancing up at the road ahead, Ragnar's heart skipped a beat. He could see the remains of an animal just a little way ahead of where he was standing. Careful to stay visible to the evening rush-hour commuters speeding past him, Ragnar strode toward the bloodied and shattered remains of the animal.

As he approached the unfortunate creature, it was clear from the fragments of shell and skin that the animal had been a tortoise, and it had been alive until only a short while ago. Although the shell was badly cracked and scuffed, Ragnar, as an avid reptile enthusiast, could identify the Chelonian as a young African Spurred tortoise, also known as a sulcata tortoise, a very common reptile in the exotic pet trade, capable of reaching between seventy-five and one hundred pounds.

A worrying thought flashed across Ragnar's mind, and he sprinted back toward the pile of discarded goods. He searched for any containers which might have once housed the sulcata. Behind the pile of aquariums, obscured by the tall, unkempt grass and barely visible were more empty carriers, broken bags of rabbit feed, and a battered cardboard box. Ragnar lifted the box onto the tarmac in order to better examine it. The box was badly worn and was crudely held together with dry, peeling duct tape. On its bleached surface were the faint outlines of the Home Depot logo, and there was a small, soggy hole in one of the bottom corners of the box.

Flicking open his utility knife, Ragnar easily sliced through the tape securing the top of the box. He pulled back the cardboard flaps and peered inside. Before his eyes could make sense of what he was seeing, the putrid smell of death erupted from the box. An acidic, acrid smell which once experienced is unmistakable and unforgettable. Scrunching up his face in disgust and taking a breath from over his shoulder, Ragnar peered back into the box. There, huddled in a small group were an assortment of tortoises of varying colours, sizes, and conditions.

Judging by the feces which lined the bottom of the box and the advanced level of decay in the deceased red-eared slider, the reptiles had been living in squalor for quite some time before being dumped.

Ragnar quickly recorded a video of the grim discovery before removing the stiff slider and placing it softly in the tall grass. "I'm so sorry, friend," he said softly as he covered the turtle's shell with bundles of colourful fall leaves.

Turning his attention back to the survivors, he counted three young sulcatas, a leopard tortoise (so named for the leopard-like rosettes on their shells), and one red-footed tortoise. Red-footed tortoises are a particularly attractive and unique looking species, with predominantly black shells, some yellow or orange markings at the tallest tips of their shells, and vibrant red and orange spots on their feet resembling paint splatters.

Realising that the young sulcata tortoise on the road had likely escaped through the hole in the corner of the box, Ragnar removed his gloves and stuffed them into the hole to create a makeshift plug.

The Detroit traffic was beginning to amass as more people began their commutes home. The cars which had been speeding past when Ragnar arrived were now crawling and coating the air with exhaust fumes. Ragnar pulled the neckline of his T-shirt up over his mouth and nose, but it did little to bring him any relief from the smog. Picking up the box of tortoises, Ragnar scanned the area one last time before heading back to the safety of his truck.

At the rescue centre, Ragnar began the process of creating a file and health records for each of the new tortoises.

Aside from being a little light and very dehydrated, the three young sulcata tortoises, all found to be males, were given a clean bill of health. The leopard tortoise, which was only the size of a small mango, still had quite a way to grow and had a beautiful buttercream shell and dark rosettes all over its carapace. Aside from some slight scabbing on its tail, likely due to being nipped at by one of the other tortoises, it, too, was found to be male and, thankfully, in reasonable condition.

The largest of the surviving tortoises was the beautiful red-foot tortoise. She alone was found to be a female, but her condition was appalling. Her beak was severely overgrown and was curling downward and back toward her throat. It would be impossible for her to eat with her beak in such an unnatural position and would need gradual and careful filing. Worst of all, her shell was not smooth and dome-shaped in the way that a healthy red-footed tortoise's shell should be. Instead, her shell was rough and stuck out in peculiar positions, giving her a crushed and lumpy look. This deformity, known as "pyramiding" in turtles, is the result of a sub-par diet and poor living conditions. It is not the kind of issue which can happen overnight.

Ragnar frowned as he lifted the lethargic red-foot up to inspect her overgrown beak. Although it was his job to care for the animals that arrived at the rescue, he was often frustrated at how avoidable so many of the animals' health issues were. Ragnar had never encountered such a deformed shell, and the sight of the tortoise's dry eyes and sweet, tired face were heartbreaking.

"I'm going to take care of you. You're safe now," said Ragnar softly as he gently traced his fingertips over the tortoise's shell.

Although a healthy tortoise's shell is made of bone and tough plates of keratin, it is not without feeling, and the female red-foot tortoise quickly drew her legs and head inwards and held them tight against her body, unused to Ragnar's affectionate touch. She huffed slightly to express her discomfort before extending her long neck out and attempting to nip at Ragnar's fingers. If her beak hadn't been so overgrown, she would have landed a hefty bite, but, instead, the most she could muster was a vicious head-butt.

Ragnar couldn't help but be impressed by the sickly tortoise's fighting spirit and gently placed her back down onto the examination table.

Over the next few weeks, each of the sulcatas and the leopard tortoise were all given a clean bill of health and adopted out to good homes, but the red-foot tortoise wouldn't be ready for adoption for a long time, if ever. Her spunky personality had become such a favourite of Ragnar's and the rest of the animal rescue team that she had become an official animal ambassador for the rescue organization. Photo updates of her journey to recovery were shared on social media, helping drive home the importance of proper animal husbandry to a global audience.

Once it was certain that she was going to survive her ordeal, she was named Bubbles as a tribute to her habit of holding her head underwater and blowing bubbles through her nostrils. Bubbles had settled into life at the centre very well and now lived in a large tortoise exhibit room where she enjoyed the company of a herd of other South American Chelonians. Her beak was slowly being trimmed back to a healthier size and she was managing to eat like a normal tortoise.

Ragnar found himself becoming ever more attached to Bubbles. The improvement in her diet and habitat began to encourage her inner diva, and she was proving to be quite a pint-sized terror. Every morning, Bubbles would wait for breakfast to arrive. She would lie motionless, buried slightly in the deep substrate, and as soon as someone would open the door, she would hoist her heavy body up and rush at full speed toward the door, eager to claim all of the tastiest foods in the breakfast fruit and vegetable salad. Being one of the larger tortoises in the exhibit, she would often use her size to her advantage and barge the smaller tortoises out of the way, sometimes with so much force that some of the smallest would be flipped upside down, waving their feet pathetically in the air until they could muster the strength to flip themselves back over.

Many of the tortoises were long-term residents and would soon lose interest in their human visitors if the humans didn't bring food into the enclosure. Bubbles, however, had begun to actively seek out human company and would rush to certain carers with glee. Bubbles's favourite carer was Ragnar. Regardless of whether he was scatter-feeding the herd, providing enrichment, coming in to spot-clean the room, or do a quick visual check of the tortoises, Bubbles would obsessively follow him around the room and gently nudge his shoes until he would pick her up and scratch her softly on her neck or her shell. She was friendly with other humans, but she wouldn't exhibit such relentless attention-seeking behaviour with anyone else. This led Ragnar to believe that Bubbles had the ability to recognise individuals and possessed enough awareness to show preference.

Ragnar had always been fascinated by the surprising cognitive abilities of animals. A few years prior to becoming a rescuer, he had worked for a time as a dog trainer, specializing in rehabilitating aggressive canines and exploring how stress thresholds impacted their behaviour.

With Bubbles showing such unexpected signs of intelligence, Ragnar found himself thinking of training methods which could prove effective for a tortoise. The idea of training a tortoise to perform a task in exchange for a reward was an exciting prospect, and he spent several sleepless nights researching Chelonian intelligence and devising a simple training plan for Bubbles.

After one particularly inspiring night of research, Ragnar excitedly flew through the colourful doors of the rescue and got straight to work on preparing the breakfast salad for the tortoises. He chopped up collard greens, carrot greens, three boiled eggs, and some apple, coating the entire mixture lightly with powdered vitamins.

Ragnar fumbled with his keys to the tortoise exhibit, their metallic clinking sound rousing the expectant and hungry occupants within. Already, Ragnar could hear the dull plodding sound of stumpy feet racing toward the door to greet him. He carefully pushed the door open and stepped over the stainless-steel barrier which prevented the tortoises from walking all the way up to the exhibit door and sustaining accidental injuries. He smiled as he was confronted with the familiar sight of the entire herd of beautifully coloured tortoises rushing toward him, their chubby faces fixated on him, eagerly awaiting their breakfast.

Bubbles, who had been soaking in the shallow heated water pond, hauled her heavy body up the AstroTurf ramp and shuffled as fast as she could toward Ragnar. Ragnar tossed the bulk of the food to one side of the enclosure and watched as the small group of tortoises climbed over and barged past one another to get to the most prized food items first. He glanced at them, subconsciously conducting a headcount and scanning them for any signs of illness. Once he was satisfied that everyone was accounted for and well, he bent down and scooped up Bubbles who was attempting to eat his sneakers, possibly mistaking the white rubber soles for boiled egg. Water dripped from her disfigured shell and ran down Ragnar's hands and forearms as he crossed the room with her and placed her gently down in a clearing, away from the rest of the herd.

Ragnar knelt down and suspended a fistful of crisp collard greens above Bubbles's head to get her attention. She lifted her head up toward the tasty greens and craned her neck as far up as she could until she was almost exclusively standing on her tough nails and beginning to lose her balance. As she continued to reach with her neck, Ragnar gently lifted one of her front feet up and said "paw." He felt slightly absurd, but he truly felt that with time and repetition, Bubbles might be able to learn this one trick.

Bubbles didn't give any indication that she had heard the vocal command or felt Ragnar lifting her foot. Instead, she simply opened her mouth and gaped, her tiny pink tongue dancing around in her mouth and her eyes completely fixated on the vegetables above her.

Ragnar lowered her foot back down, said "Yes!" and offered her a few bites of the greens as a reward.

Ragnar repeated the exercise several times, but the results were very much as he had predicted this first training session to be. There was no reaction from Bubbles or any sort of indication that she was processing any information.

The rest of the day was entirely ordinary. The morning shift was a steady conveyor belt of unwanted and abandoned animals being dropped at the rescue. The first animals to be received were three vocal and starving guinea pigs whose human family had lost interest in them. The wood shavings in their small mass-produced plastic hutch were a deep orange and smelled strongly of urine. Their feet were red and raw from standing in their own waste, and their teeth desperately needed to be trimmed.

The afternoon was also blur of application forms, surrenders, and phone calls, but thankfully a handful of animals in need of homes were matched and placed with loving new families.

Among the animals leaving to go to their new homes was a blind, deaf, and diabetic white cat called Sir. Sir had been overlooked by potential families for months due to his need for lifelong medication.

Sir's relinquishment had been particularly difficult. He had been well loved by an elderly woman for almost twenty years but had been reluctantly surrendered to the rescue when his owner was moved into a care home. Ragnar felt a wave of happiness and gratitude wash over him as Sir was lovingly carried out of the rescue by a kind woman who had just lost her own senior kitten to old age and was looking to provide a calm home for another. Ragnar was certain that Sir, whose mission was simply to find a warm lap to take naps on, would be well loved and doted on with his new family.

As the sun faded away, leaving in its wake a biting chill, Ragnar wished his colleagues a good night and began to close of the rescue. The dull hum of Detroit rush-hour traffic sitting at a standstill on the road outside prompted Ragnar to slow his pace. His time was better spent getting a head start on tomorrow's work rather than sitting in traffic.

He sat down in the administrator's chair and was about to begin printing out new adoption forms when he remembered that he'd forgotten to switch on the night lights in the tortoise room.

Ragnar wound his way through the vibrant animal print-themed corridors, stopping in at the kitchen to grab a handful of mustard greens before visiting the tortoises. As usual, Ragnar's keys caused the entire herd to begin racing as fast as possible toward the enclosure door. As Ragnar entered, he flicked on the red nighttime bulbs and glanced down at the floor, expecting to see Bubbles. His heart sank for a moment as he checked around the door guard and in the foliage near the front of the enclosure. Ragnar glanced toward the back of the enclosure and breathed a sigh of relief. There, some twenty feet away, Bubbles was contentedly waiting in the spot that they had been working in that morning. Her head was held high, and, although she had tiny eyes, it was clear that they were fixated on Ragnar's hands.

Ragnar scattered some of the mustard greens at the front of the enclosure before carefully making his way around the soaking pond and over to Bubbles. Ragnar crouched down and gently scratched the area of shell just above Bubbles's tail, making her swing her hind quarters from side to side.

Ragnar felt his stomach grumble as held out the greens in his hand and raised them above Bubbles's head. He was eager to make their training session as quick as possible so that he could continue the shutdown of the centre and head home. Ragnar reached toward the hungry tortoise with his free hand.

"Paw," he said, ready to lift her front foot up for her and reward her, but, before he could touch her foot, it quite unexpectedly shot upwards until it was suspended outwards at her shoulder height.

Ragnar was in complete disbelief. A fruit fly landed on his lip and made him all too aware that his mouth had fallen open in shock. He exhaled sharply and shook his head, sloughing off the tiny fly. Ragnar praised Bubbles vocally before giving her the small bundle of greens in his hand.

Bubbles relaxed her thick, stubby foot back down on the floor and began munching on her prize.

Ragnar could hardly bring himself to believe that Bubbles had retained their morning training. At the time, she hadn't given any indication that she had understood that she was being taught a behaviour. Ragnar's knees were beginning to ache with stiffness, and they clicked as he straightened and crossed back toward the enclosure door. He decided to remain sceptical for the moment, choosing to believe that Bubbles may have simply been stretching, or that perhaps she was about to take a step forward, but lost focus or changed her mind.

His mind continued to race as he drove through the city, passing the blue lights of the GM Renaissance Center

and thinking of Bubbles's red spots each time he sat at a
traffic light.

The following day, Ragnar power-walked into the reception
area of the rescue, his coat soaked by the cold rain. He
was over an hour late from having to detour around a
flooded street.

At the front desk, glancing over some volunteer application
forms, was Kelly, the founder of the rescue.

Kelly was a commanding presence. She had black hair cut
sharply into a perfect chin-length bob and teal 1950s style
bangs. Her faux-tortoiseshell glasses contrasted against
her pale skin, and, despite being in her mid-thirties, she
had as much animal rescue experience as some rehabbers
twice her age.

Ragnar felt guilty that he was late to work. The centre was
going through a period of being understaffed, and any
absence was felt by the whole team who were constantly
stretched thin.

"Sorry I'm late. Has anyone fed the tortoises their veggie chop
yet?" he asked as he loosened the scarf from around his neck
and smoothed down his beard which was sparkling from
the raindrops.

"Yes, I think Charlie has just finished with the reptiles. She found that corn snake which escaped last week. He's totally fine. She saw him slither under the refrigerator and managed to coax him out. Isn't it funny how they always go toward the kitchen appliances? It must be the heat that attracts them." Kelly continued to flick quickly through the volunteer application forms.

Ragnar was a little disheartened that the tortoises had already been fed. He had hoped to sneak in a training session with Bubbles while she was motivated by hunger.

"Oh, that's great about the corn. I was beginning to worry with winter being a few weeks away. If you don't need me to drive out for a pick-up, I'll get started on the small mammal diets and—"

"Ragnar?" interrupted Kelly. She peered up at him knowingly through the clear lenses of her cat-eye glasses.

"What were you getting up to with the tortoises last night? I saw you on the live tortoise webcam." Kelly wiggled her phone at Ragnar, reminding him that she had a surveillance app on her phone. She wasn't being accusatory, but she did speak with a hint of concern.

Ragnar held his breath for a moment as he tried to think of the best way to explain to Kelly his recent actions.

"Actually," he sighed, "I'm trying to train one of the tortoises." He shrank internally, realising how crazy he must sound.

"You're...training a tortoise?" repeated Kelly, doing her best to sound understanding and intrigued. She raised her "Best Cat Mom" mug to her lips and took a sip of coffee, never dropping her gaze from Ragnar.

Ragnar shrugged his shoulders. "I know it sounds crazy, but I think that tortoises can recognise individuals and might have the ability to learn basic tricks."

Kelly couldn't contain herself any longer. She snorted into her mug, the heat from the coffee instantly fogging up her glasses.

Ragnar smiled an uncertain, queasy smile. He wasn't sure if he was being ridiculed or about to be placed on mandatory bed rest.

As Kelly continued to cackle and snort uncontrollably, the door to the staff area opened and Jess glided into the reception area. Jess owned her own dog grooming business but donated a few days per month to washing and grooming the centre's rescue dogs. For a moment, Ragnar was completely oblivious to Kelly's laughter. He glanced sideways over at Jess, who was cradling a newly groomed Havanese.

Jess had an alluring, vampiric sort of beauty with pale skin, red lips, dark chocolate brown hair, and arctic blue eyes. Ragnar always found himself incapable of forming coherent sentences around her. He experienced a flashback to their last disastrous encounter when Jess had asked him about his weekend. He had opened his mouth in an attempt to respond, but he couldn't make a sound. Instead, he managed to form a saliva bubble, which protruded out of his mouth just enough for Jess to witness it, before it popped and left Ragnar wishing that the ground would swallow him up. The trauma of that embarrassment was weeks ago, but Ragnar still cringed into his pillow at night whenever he thought of her.

Jess looked from Ragnar, who was still dripping rain onto the reception floor, to Kelly, who was now wheezing uncontrollably at the front desk, smacking her hand on her thigh.

"Clearly, I just missed out on a very good joke," said Jess, looking over at Ragnar and raising one of her perfect, Instagram-worthy eyebrows.

Kelly coughed and spluttered, looking over at Jess.

"You bet you did! Ragnar was just telling me that his new hobby is tortoise training!"

Ragnar felt his neck begin to redden and his heart began to race. He adored Kelly, but she really didn't have any tact. And it wasn't exactly a hobby. It was scientific research!

Jess glanced back over at Ragnar, swirling her fingers in the Havanese's perfectly groomed fur. She could see him beginning to flush and realised how uncomfortable he must be feeling.

"Really?" exclaimed Jess brightly. "I think that's amazing! I didn't know that you could train tortoises," she said, flashing Ragnar a congenial smile.

"You can't!" exclaimed Kelly, wiping an eyeliner-stained tear away. "Unless they're digging out of their enclosures, tortoises don't perform tricks."

"Actually, Bubbles is already showing signs that she's responding well to the training," said Ragnar, doing his best not to sound indignant.

Kelly straightened up in her seat, still reeling quietly at the vision she conjured in her head of Ragnar training the tortoises to roll over and jump through hoops.

"Ragnar, you're a great trainer. Brilliant, in fact, but I just don't see how you can train a tortoise. They're simply not intelligent enough. Crocodilians and some lizard species are incredibly intelligent, but not turtles. Maybe at a stretch you might have some luck with the larger Chelonian species, like Galapagos or Aldabra tortoises, but these smaller species... they're a little more basic and survival-driven."

Ragnar shook his head and scratched the back of his neck.

"I disagree. I have reason to believe that tortoises have the mental capacity to recognise their caregivers and perform basic tasks in order to receive a reward. I'm working with Bubbles, and after only one session she is showing signs that she is retaining her training."

The low buzz of the air purifier seemed deafening as Ragnar waited for a response. The red light on the reception phone began to blink, indicating that someone had left a message on the answering machine.

Kelly glanced down at the telephone instinctively before reaching across the desk for a pen.

"OK, Ragnar. If you can prove to me that one of your shell-buddies can learn a trick, I'll give you fifty dollars. If you're unsuccessful, you have to pay me fifty dollars and answer the telephone voicemails for a week." Kelly extended her hand out for Ragnar and shot him a cocky smile.

Jess rolled her eyes and chuckled as Ragnar strode over to Kelly and shook her hand.

"You better get fifty bucks ready for me, Kelly. You'll be handing it over to me in less than a week!"

***

Ragnar had expected that it might take a few days, or possibly even a few weeks before Bubbles might show signs that she truly understood their training, but as Ragnar placed the excitable little tortoise down in the clearing of the exhibit, he noticed that just as with the previous night, Bubbles was taking the initiative to raise her front foot, impatiently gaping her mouth and appealing for food.

It was inconceivable that Bubbles could have retained any training from the previous day after only two short sessions, but here she was, anticipating what might be asked of her and knowing that if she performed this task, she would likely receive a reward. Ragnar crouched down and scratched his long red beard. Bubbles stared up at him, still lifting and moving her front leg around in a clumsy waving motion.

"Paw," said Ragnar as he extended his hand toward Bubbles. She immediately lifted her front left foot even higher and bumped it against his hand.

Ragnar gave her vocal praise and dropped a slice of strawberry into her mouth. Bubbles gleefully began to massacre the strawberry, reducing the fruit to a gloopy paste which covered her mouth and dripped off of her beak.

Bubbles continued to surprise Ragnar over the next few days, eagerly focusing on him and raising her foot time and time again for a treat. Ragnar had begun to document her training progress on his phone, hopeful that one day he might be able to share his findings with herpetological and zoological professionals.

On Friday, six days after they had first begun their training, Ragnar entered the tortoise enclosure once again, eager to fit in one last training session before the weekend, when he was not scheduled to work.

Bubbles and the rest of the herd all rushed toward him, anticipating the blueberries and kale which he had in a small feeding dish. Ragnar knelt down to feed a blueberry to one of the smallest yellow-foot tortoises when Bubbles pushed in front of him and waved her foot wildly, desperate to eat the first blueberry.

Ragnar withdrew his hand from the smaller tortoise and gave the plump blueberry to Bubbles. She happily devoured the fruit, nudging away the other jealous tortoises. Ragnar watched fondly as Bubbles slurped away at the berry.

Ragnar reached into the treat bowl and plucked out another blueberry. As he crouched down and lowered it toward the smallest tortoise, the little tortoise raised one of its tough yellow spotted feet and promptly rested it back on the floor. This happened so quickly that Ragnar barely had time to register what had occurred. Had the smallest tortoise in the group observed that Bubbles was given a treat ahead of him as she performed a foot lift?

Ragnar tore some kale out of the bowl and held it above the smallest tortoise. "Paw" he said clearly, holding his hand out and holding the food above his head.

Bubbles, who had finished her berry and was now eyeing the kale in his hand, began furiously waving. Ragnar reached over and gave her a small nibble. Almost immediately after her, the small yellow-foot also began to wave once more.

As Ragnar praised the little tortoise, another red-foot, slightly smaller than Bubbles, also lifted her leg and began to wave. Soon, all of the tortoises in the room were taking turns waving for attention and waiting for treats.

Ragnar couldn't believe his eyes. He set down his phone and began recording the entire session, realising what a significant breakthrough this research could be.

***

Ragnar was scarcely ever able to enjoy a full weekend off from work. Usually his weekends would be interrupted to perform an emergency rescue, but as Kelly had recently hired more weekend drivers, Ragnar was able to take his first full weekend off in months.

The weather was mild for mid-November, and the sky was a cerulean blue without a single cloud, the perfect weather for hiking, but Ragnar couldn't enjoy himself. He was obsessing over his previous week's work in the tortoise exhibit, and a million questions and ideas raced through his mind.

One question in particular was haunting his thoughts: would the tortoises remember their training over the weekend, or would they forget? It was all he could do to stop himself from giving up on his weekend and dropping in at the centre to check in on the herd which he was now so fond of.

***

On Monday morning, Ragnar was the first to arrive at the centre. He had been eager to arrive early and give himself extra time to train the tortoises before starting his regular duties. As he pulled into a parking space, his heart began to sink as he saw three cardboard boxes piled against the doors. With the holidays just around corner, it was typical for the rescue to receive old and unwanted pets to make way for newer, younger animals.

He parked quickly and rushed over to the boxes. Detroit was already bitterly cold at this time of year, and if any abandoned animals had been sitting out in poorly insulated boxes overnight, they could be suffering from hypothermia or worse.

Ragnar used his truck key to slice open the tape on one of the boxes, carefully pulling back the flaps and peering inside. He breathed a sigh of relief as he saw donations of hay, rabbit pellets, and vitamin blocks. He quickly sliced open the other two boxes, worried that there may be an abandoned rabbit but was grateful to find that one contained an ample supply of kitty litter and the other was full to the brim with dog kibble.

He unlocked the doors to the centre and dragged the boxes inside, leaving them in the reception areas for one of the trainee volunteers to sort through and put away.

Ragnar quickly devoured a banana from the employee room and took another to use as a motivational incentive for the tortoises.

Ragnar entered the room, elated to see the group of happy, bright-eyed tortoises. He knelt on the floor, his knees sinking into the jungle bark and soil mixture which covered the floor, and placed his camera on the ground, ready to record his session. From the far side of the exhibit, Bubbles was racing toward him, a little crown of dirt balancing on her head from where she had spent the night buried lightly in the ground.

***

Ragnar was contentedly sipping at his warm butternut squash soup in the employee room when Kelly and Charlie, one of the few other permanent staff members, joined him with their lunches.

Kelly's bangs were now dyed hot pink, and Charlie, by contrast, was a petite, blonde bombshell whose first and only love was amphibians.

Charlie and Kelly were close friends outside of the rescue and were excitedly chatting together, making plans for a girls' weekend in New Orleans.

Ragnar glanced up, acknowledging them as they sat down at the table.

Kelly smirked playfully and unwrapped her smoked salmon and cream cheese bagel.

"So, Ragnar, how are things going?" she teased. "Are you having any success training your army of tortoises?"

Ragnar smiled into his soup.

"You should come by before closing and see for yourself," he replied. "Unless you're too chicken?"

Kelly and Charlie exchanged glances with one another. Kelly looked back at Ragnar and took a slow bite of her bagel, closing her eyes in deep, dramatic pleasure as she slowly chewed her mouthful.

She took her time swallowing before meeting Ragnar's gaze again.

"You're about to buy my bagels for the next month. Get ready to kiss fifty dollars goodbye," she said confidently.

Only a handful of employee vehicles remained in the parking lot as evening fell and the centre closed its doors to the public.

Ragnar was crouched down in the warm, humid tortoise enclosure, with Kelly and Charlie paying close attention behind him.

Bubbles, with her wonky shell, plodded cheerfully over to Ragnar, gazing up at him patiently. In his hand, he held the epitome of all treats, a juicy, protein-rich superworm. As he had done countless times in the past week, he extended the treat over Bubbles's head. Her mouth immediately opened wide, and she began to stretch her neck upwards.

"Paw," said Ragnar, as he extended his hand out to her.

Right on cue, Bubbles lifted her foot up and placed it without hesitation in Ragnar's hand. Both Kelly and Charlie were left speechless as they watched Ragnar praise the tortoise and reward her with the worm.

The other tortoises, who had lost interest in the trio of humans when they realised that they didn't come bearing any gifts of fruit or vegetables, began to smell the buttery superworm and were quick to double back toward the door. When motivated with live invertebrates, the tortoises could move at a surprisingly fast pace. The sight was comical, like watching a race between cheap wind-up toys from the dollar store.

Soon, Bubbles was joined by half a dozen more tortoises, each raising one of their front feet with varying degrees of success.

Kelly tried her best to form a sentence, but she could scarcely make a sound.

"Amazing," she said breathlessly as she crouched down next to Ragnar.

"They haven't tried this with anyone else," said Ragnar as he handed Kelly a worm. "But I think they're intelligent enough to perform this trick for anyone holding a treat."

Kelly gently pinched the thrashing superworm between her fingers. Its shiny body contorted as it attempted to bite her finger, but it only made contact with her tough fingernail. Oblivious to the superworm's struggle, Kelly held out her hand above the head of a smaller red-foot stationed right in front of her.

"Paw," she said, feeling a little ridiculous.

The tortoise swayed slightly on the spot, before lifting and replacing its foot quickly. Almost immediately, the other tortoises began to wave, until they looked almost like a troop of lucky money cats.

Behind Kelly and Ragnar, Charlie was bewitched by the peculiar sight.

"Incredible!" she whispered.

"I've been filming their progress for a week," said Ragnar, offering another superworm to Bubbles.

"I was only planning to work with Bubbles, but the others observed her and caught on quickly."

Ragnar deposited another superworm into Bubbles's mouth and cringed as she bit it in half and savoured its juices.

In the reception area, Jess was finishing up her report for the day's visit. She had decided to come in briefly to clip all of the dogs' nails. Loud, excitable voices coming from the hallway made Jess look up. She quickly checked her appearance in the reflection of the computer and fluffed her hair.

The door swung forward, and Kelly, Charlie, and Ragnar all poured into the reception area, conversing about what they had witnessed together in the tortoise room. Kelly crossed behind the desk and reached into a drawer where she kept her personal belongings.

"As much as I hate to say it, you were right, Ragnar. I think you're onto something special," she said, as she pulled out two twenty dollar bills and a ten.

Ragnar stepped backward and shook his head. He didn't want to accept Kelly's money but Kelly scowled and insisted.

"A deal is a deal, Ragnar. We shook on it. Besides, I'll be winning that back again when you try to teach some of the new cats how to use a litter tray!"

Ragnar smiled and nodded, accepting his winnings from Kelly.

Kelly glanced at Jess and gave a sly smile to Ragnar as she handed him the bills. "That new restaurant, Gino's, just opened a few blocks down. The reviews are good. You should treat Jess to some dinner."

Ragnar felt his ears begin to burn and turn red. Once again, he had been blindsided by Kelly's complete lack of tact.

Jess seized the opportunity to be brave.

"I'd actually really like that. I'm starving!"

***

Jess climbed up into Ragnar's truck.

She was impressed with how clean the vehicle was and noted that the air freshener was cherry scented, her favourite. Ragnar, who was starting the car to get some heat going did an internal fist pump, thanking himself for cleaning his car the day before and for impulse purchasing a random air freshener from the gas station.

"So you really did it?" asked Jess as she began to buckle herself. "You really managed to find a way to train tortoises?"

Ragnar looked over at Jess buckling herself into the seat. The reflection of the streetlights on her face made her eyes look like fireplaces. She looked over to Ragnar, waiting for him to reply. He gulped, only to find that his mouth and throat were very dry. Mustering up his courage he lifted his phone and placed it on his dashboard.

"Yes, I guess I did. Maybe after dinner I could show you some of the training videos I took on my 'shellphone'?"

A fleeting moment of silence passed between them before Jess howled with laughter. Ragnar breathed a sigh of relief and shifted his truck into drive.

"Actually" replied Jess, "I would turtley love that! Let's go and shellebrate."

Tortoise Facts 🐢

- A group of tortoises is actually called a "creep."

- A turtle's shell is part of its skeleton and includes its rib cage and spine.

- The part of a turtle's shell on its back is called the carapace, and the shell underneath is called a plastron. The scales on the carapace are called scutes.

- Alligator snapping turtles have been recorded to have a bite force of over a thousand pounds.

- The current record holder for the oldest living tortoise is Jonathan. In 2019, he turned 187 years old.

- Turtles live in or near bodies of water, whereas tortoises live on land. Fully aquatic turtles like the loggerhead sea turtle have paddle-shaped arms and feet to help them glide through the water. A turtle or terrapin is most likely to have partially webbed and clawed feet, suitable for gripping lake and riverbeds or climbing up onto rocks. Tortoises have broad feet and are often armed with tough nails that are perfect tools for digging.

- In some species, you tell if a tortoise is male or female judging by the shape of their plastron. If its flat, the animal is female. If it curves inwards, the specimen is likely to be male.

BEAR

"It's quite simple."

The doctor pulled his eyes away from his ancient yellowing computer and swivelled in his leather chair to look at me.

"What it really comes down to is whether or not you want to effectively manage your condition. I strongly advise you to consider exploring medication. I can assure you that it is a very safe option."

Medication. That word, though spoken so mundanely by the doctor, somehow managed to permeate my skin and freeze me to my core. I shifted in my chair uncomfortably.

Sensing my discontent, the doctor sighed and turned back to his computer where he typed a few words in my patient notes.

Outside, the heavy raindrops were beating down on the parked cars, sounding like the hum of radio static. The pattering of rain, usually so pleasing to my ears, did nothing to muffle the increased volume of my heartbeat.

Looking down at the stained, green carpet in the office, I focused on the rigid body of a deceased house fly. Its legs contorted into a prayer position. I wondered if it had died of natural causes or whether it had collided one too many times with the window above it in a bid to free itself from such an overwhelmingly depressing office.

"What would you like to do, Emma?"

I cringed a little at the use of my full first name. It was 2018 and nobody had called me "Emma" since I was in school over a decade ago. I typically associated my full name with being scolded by teachers or my mother.

"Emma?" The doctor inquired again with a hint of impatience.

"I'll figure it out myself," I replied unconvincingly.

The doctor peered over his glasses at me. "You understand that, as a condition, Bipolar Disorder cannot be cured, but it can be managed with some help. I strongly suggest CBT therapy, paired with some antidep–"

"I understand, doctor. I'll manage. Thanks for seeing me."

Walking the few streets back to my North London flat, I distracted myself from my thoughts by watching strangers seek shelter from the April showers, some hiding under soggy newspapers and others strolling quickly under the protection of their umbrellas, their faces illuminated by their mobile phones.

The quiet of my bright, airy home was often my sanctuary where I could rest and recover, but it could also be a self-inflicted prison. Over the years, I had spent countless blurry months, hardly aware of my own existence, sitting with my back against the warm radiator, functioning just enough to motivate myself to go to work or nibble on a £3.00 meal deal from Sainsbury's.

I dried myself off from the rain and settled on the sofa with a drink to review my flight back to New Jersey. I had hastily moved to the USA six months prior, which already seemed like a lifetime ago.

At the time of my move, people had assumed that I was making the jump across the pond to aid my rapidly growing career as a digital animal educator on YouTube. Others saw my relocation as the natural progression of my transatlantic relationship with Danny, my boyfriend of several years. In fact, my rushed move to America was less of an exciting level-up and more of a desperate attempt to distance myself from a series of emotional and psychological traumas, the last of which giving me the ultimate push to leave my UK home.

I sipped at my drink—warm apple and black currant squash—and thought back over the doctor's recommendation of trying antidepressants. I had seen friends of mine lose their ability to cry or sleep after committing to antidepressants. I had also witnessed firsthand in an ex-boyfriend of mine how limiting and severe antidepressant dependency could be. The thought of medicating myself in any way or artificially altering the chemical balance of my body was a terrifying prospect, a sort of unnecessary self-zombifying. If there was anything I was certain of, it was that I would not be taking antidepressants.

Glancing up, I looked out toward the corridor which ran alongside my living room. I had thought for a moment that I'd seen a little flash of white dash across the hallway. I smiled into my drink and remembered my little best friend, Bear.

For seven years prior to my move to the USA, I had been happily working in various capacities for an animal education company, bringing all manner of animals into schools, special needs groups, and community events. My colleagues were captivating birds of prey, mischievous meerkats, beautiful reptiles, Indian fruit bats (some the size of bowling pins), a huge variety of invertebrates, and my favourite animal of all, my pet ferret, Bear. Bear was an albino ferret of unrivalled proportions. He had huge burgundy eyes and a tubular, muscular body. A friend of mine had bred and raised Bear to be a rabbiting ferret. His job was to venture down into rabbit warrens and flush out the quarry within. The rabbits would then be captured

and humanely dispatched, which helped to safeguard
agricultural crops.

 Bear's mother was a champion
rabbit flusher. Having come from
a long line of hunting stock, it was
believed that Bear would also be
an exemplary rabbiter. However,
he grew far too large, docile, and
lazy for his intended purpose, and
so was gifted to me as an animal
ambassador for my educational
presentations. At this job, Bear
excelled! I would present loud,
large, and rare exotic species to audiences, but Bear's mellow
personality and warm, chubby belly stole hearts again and
again. He was often requested for an encore at the end of my
presentations, overshadowing crocodilians, giant snakes, and
even the absurdly fluffy chinchillas.

For my last few years in London before I moved to the
USA, Bear was often my only companion. My work hours
as a mobile animal educator were hideously unsociable.
During my busiest months, I would wake up at three thirty
in the morning to drive to work to clean, feed, and pack
the animals, ready for a day of educational shows. By the
time I finished work (often in several different parts of the

southeast of England), settled the animals back at the facility and driven home, it could be anywhere between seven and eleven thirty at night. Bear was often my only affection and company during these times.

Ferrets are often stigmatized as being aggressive creatures with a pungent odour. In truth, the vast majority of ferrets are extremely playful and sweet when properly socialized. However, their reputation for being somewhat fragrant is quite well deserved!

At home, Bear would amuse me endlessly with his playful antics. His favourite game was to daintily take any item I handed to him (usually a brand of dog biscuit which I kept a supply of specifically because Bear enjoyed carrying them) and quickly scuttle away to stash his loot in the boiler closet. The boiler closet was Bear's favourite hang-out spot, and he would diligently arrange and rearrange his hoarded treasures for hours.

Bear was also what I would describe as my "soul animal," an animal with whom I shared an uncommonly deep bond and spiritual connection. The kind of connection which transcends both language and species and which is a true representation of a mutually enjoyed, human and animal friendship. I found Bear to be unexpectedly sentient for such a relatively small creature. He had an undeniable instinct for sensing my emotions, and he comforted me during some of my life's darkest and most hopeless moments.

Early one cold, March morning, I had been walking a number of dogs on the Hampstead Heath extension, a beautiful expanse of public parkland and fields in the heart of London. Walking my familiar route, I noticed a tree which had a strange mass suspended from it. Initially, I thought that some tarpaulin had blown into the branches and become tangled or that some teenagers had set up a makeshift swing or a hammock. However, as I approached the tree and my eyes were able to focus on the unfamiliar mass, an immediate, paralyzing cold enveloped me.

There, hanging by a makeshift noose from the tree were the remains of a man. Unable to look away, my eyes burned this man's image into my memory. His navy, mud-stained weatherproof jacket, his khaki hiking trousers, and the purple and burgundy of his hands where blood settled and pooled once his heart stopped beating.

I had with me that day a particularly playful French bulldog named Phoebe. She bounded up to the man, excitedly grunting and snorting. Seeing her wriggle excitedly and prancing underneath the man, play-bowing at his body and enticing him to throw her favourite rubber stick woke me from my frozen state.

"Phoebe, come!"

Recalling all of my dogs and tethering them to a nearby bench, I heard the distant, building sound of rush-hour traffic. I realised that school children would soon begin walking down this path on their way to nearby schools, and I quickly fumbled for my phone and dialled for police assistance.

I stayed with the body to help the emergency services find our location in the expanse of the park, and I chose my words carefully with several parents to direct them to take an alternative walking route through the park to ensure that no child should see what I had.

Waiting for police didn't take very long, perhaps only ten minutes, but, in that time, I named the man Tom. I told him how sorry I was that he felt so lonely or hopeless, and I was grateful that despite my own past traumas, I had never felt what this man must have at the time he chose to end his suffering.

For the rest of the day, I stayed indoors with my walking clients. All of the dogs sensed that it was a day for calm energy, rather than their usual rambunctiousness. Gently playing with Phoebe's velvety ears and a Yorkipoo's curly coat, I closed my eyes and allowed myself an uncharacteristic recovery nap.

For the months that followed, I would have the same reoccurring nightmare of Tom in his last desperate moments. I would call out to him and beg him not to jump, but he would never listen or make any indication that he could hear me. The dream always ended with him stepping off the tree branch, and I would wake as the dull sound of his body pulled the noose rope tight.

On the many nights that I jolted awake from this nightmare, I would peel Bear from his favourite hammock, hold him in my arms, and inhale his musty scent deep into my lungs. His familiar smell, though so offensive to some, would instantly warm and comfort me in all of the places that rounds of therapy couldn't.

I tried speaking with friends about the ordeal, but most were unable to relate to such an awful story, and others seemed only interested in morbid details. I had also spoken with special police councillors who would check in on me from time to time in the weeks following that morning in the park, but not even they could prevent the reoccurring nightmares I had of my subconscious fabrications of the last moments of Tom's life.

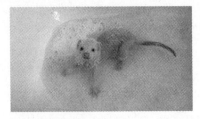

Bear, my ever-present and silent companion, was my rock.

Just as the shock of my ordeal with Tom began to fade into a benign memory, I would once again have my world tilted off its axis. Bear would be there to comfort me through the devastating loss of my baby.

Danny and I had not been planning for any children. Being in a long distance, transatlantic relationship was hardly the ideal scenario for starting a family, but our regular contraception had failed, as had the emergency contraception. Despite my initial shock, I had found myself musing at how true the saying was that nature finds a way.

As much as I was unprepared for motherhood and unwilling to sacrifice my career, the blow of my doctor's words that my baby was no longer alive at nine weeks old was devastating. The doctor ordered me to have a medical termination, which would allow me to miscarry at home in a predictable timeframe rather than allowing my body the opportunity to have a missed miscarriage.

Three months after my home miscarriage, I unexpectedly began heavily bleeding again, and I was rushed to hospital. I vaguely remember looking up at the flashing blue lights of the ambulance and seeing the light illuminate the sleet whirling around in the night air. In my dazed state, I remember thinking how pretty the sight was. I had used the last of my strength and awareness to leave copious amounts of fresh food and water for my beloved Bear as the paramedics pushed through the door to my flat and coaxed me into the ambulance. Glancing back at Bear's confused face, I vowed to be back the next day.

It was the thought of Bear at home alone that made me eat the hospital food so heartily. I wanted so much to hurry home to him that I didn't allow myself to dwell on the previous night's unexpected trauma. My operation to remove the debris of my incomplete miscarriage had been a success, and despite having slightly low blood pressure, the doctor discharged me and I hurried home in a black taxi to grieve quietly and lavish affection on my sweet little Bear.

The trauma of losing my pregnancy would be the last hardship which Bear could see me through. He was beginning to show his age and would find it increasingly difficult to maintain a healthy weight. His usually plush white winter coat was wiry and yellow. He played less, preferring instead to sleep as much as he could. During his waking minutes, he'd seek out my company and gesture to be lifted into my lap, where he'd lie contentedly and push his lemon-sized head against my palm as I gently squeezed and scratched his head, cheeks, and ears.

A piece of my soul fractured irreparably the night I had to put Bear to sleep. He was so very tired and almost completely unable to get up from his bed. Leading up to his final vet appointment, I carried him around in his little hammock, and we said goodbye to the lizards and snakes which lived in my bedroom.

I held him and spoke to him softly as we watched a final film together, and I thanked him endlessly for all of the comfort he brought me over the years.

When the time comes, some owners cannot stand to be in the room as their pets are put into their final sleep, but I wouldn't leave Bear in his final hour of need, as he had been so steadfast through so many of mine. The vet's office was warm and quiet, and I kissed him softly all over his nose as he lay in his favourite sky blue fleecy bed lined with a T-shirt of mine. I told him that it was okay for him to go to sleep and that I was sorry that my love wasn't enough to keep him alive.

The vet, a kind and compassionate woman whom I'd
entrusted with my animals' care over the years, shed a small
tear as she administered the bright blue liquid to Bear. He
did not flinch or show any sign of discomfort or pain. I kept
my face close to his in his final moments, and in a final act
to comfort me, he lifted his head with immense difficulty one
last time to lick a tear from my nose before exhaling into his
eternal rest.

Losing Bear affected me on what felt like a molecular level.
I felt that every part of me was less than it had been before
his passing.

***

Moving to America coincided with a sudden explosion of
growth of my YouTube channel. I spent my days filming and
editing as much as I possibly could to keep my mind busy
and away from London.

By night, I celebrated my reunion with Danny and finally being
able to live our lives in close proximity and in a shared space.

Danny, a zoologist and an animal educator like myself,
had his own array of animal ambassadors which kept me
occupied and living in the present. His laughing Kookaburra
named Babakook would prove to be the first animal I
encountered who would hate the sight of me. If we were in

the same room together, or if I walked into his aviary, I'd
have to protect my eyes and head at all times as he tried to
spear my face with his huge, powerful beak. In a strange way,
his hatred was a refreshing breath of honesty.

Kaa, my royal python from London, had arrived in America
several weeks before I had and was already settled and
enjoying life in New Jersey. Her presence, though a huge
sense of warmth and familiarity to me, was a reminder of the
hopes I once had that I would bring Bear with me to America.
I missed him greatly during my first few months.

On YouTube, my channel continued to grow at a rapid pace. I
was so proud of the positive community of animal lovers that
my channel was nurturing. Seeing the comments sections
of my videos filled with viewers and fans helping each other
with pet care and animal questions gave me such elation
that I continued to work hard and churn out at least one
video per week.

A common comment I would receive (and still do) is that I
am a hugely positive person and that others find this trait
of mine inspiring. At times, I would read these comments
and feel like a fraud, because being cheerful wasn't always
just a result of my (usually) good nature. Although I didn't
understand it during my first few months in the USA, I
periodically experience what is described in Bipolar 2 as

"hypomania": periods of increased activity with extreme moods of elation, feelings of invincibility, and grandiosity, paired with risk taking and a significantly decreased need for sleep.

At the time, I had not yet been diagnosed with Bipolar 2, so it was impossible for me to heed the warning signs of a hypomania episode. However, with every up, there comes a down, and with Bipolar 2, my occasional lows are prolonged periods of inactivity where it can be extremely difficult to stay awake for more than an hour at a time. Becoming a social hermit, overeating the wrong foods, and falling into a deep depression are all par for the course.

Multiple times in my life, I have experienced both episodes, always after a huge change or upset in my life.

In hindsight, moving to America was less of a wonderful adventure and more of a ticking time bomb for my mental health. I had run far away from London, believing that it was the source of my grief, and ignored the uncomfortable truth that grief cannot be discarded or hidden from.

I stepped off the plane at Newark Liberty airport and instantly into a partnership with another human, a new country, a new living situation, and, possibly most drastic of all, the role of stepparent for three children from Danny's previous marriage.

As much as I piled my work plate high with projects, and no matter how many YouTube subscribers flooded to my channel with sweet words of praise, I could never find balance or peace, and, for the first time in my life, at age twenty-eight, I secretly began taking razor blades to my legs as an unhealthy coping mechanism to momentarily eliminate the overwhelming noise and prolonged implosion happening in my head.

Much to Danny's dismay, I hid away for weeks on end, barely functioning and finding no joy in what I normally would. Hours would slip past me and I uncharacteristically began sipping alcohol at night to help me sleep. Alcohol has always been a substance which I have avoided like the plague, as my body has great difficulty in digesting and processing it in any form, be it as a cocktail or even in a chocolate liqueur. The taste of alcohol is highly offensive to my mouth, and yet, I'd find myself feeding the nocturnal animals at night and then reluctantly sipping down a few teaspoons of wine to ease me into sleep.

My breaking point or "rock bottom" moment came in the autumn of 2018. I was newly engaged to Danny and was generally feeling okay after a successful summer of creating content.

The last thing I remember on that particular night was an overwhelming feeling of hopelessness. All of my anger, grief, stress, and confusion over a million unrelated things finally pushed me to my limit. I somehow managed to drink a huge bottle of wine when I'd only ever managed a sip or two of any drink before. In a state of mental apathy, I also raided the medicine cabinet.

Whether it was hours or minutes which passed as I slipped in and out of consciousness, I couldn't say, but over and over, I relived my nightmare of Tom, the man who I had found hanging in the park. The hopeless finality of his choice to end his life weighed down on my entire body like a two-ton weight, and from somewhere far away I could hear myself screaming at Tom to stop jumping. My mind played the same final, heart-stopping moments of Tom's life again and again.

Danny pushed through the bathroom door to find me unconscious sometime later. I vaguely remember his distraught voice as he picked me up off the floor which was covered in a mixture of wine, sweat, and blood from the cuts on my legs. His desperate attempts to revive me sounded as though someone was calling my name from afar. I tried to respond to him, but my mouth was incapable of making a sound. Danny checked my pulse and cleared my mouth of a build-up of froth. He slapped my arms and face to bring me back to consciousness. Spitting up some wine, I managed

to beg him not to call an ambulance. I couldn't face having
to explain myself to doctors. I cried more than I had ever
cried before in my life at how close I had come to following
Tom past the point of no return. I thought of my family,
Danny's children, my animals, and the future I was hoping
to build to help unwanted pets and those with special needs.
I could have thrown all of that away in one unmanaged
depressive episode.

Danny hushed me and listened as I poured my heart out
for the first time in years. He stayed by my bedside all
night with one of my closest girlfriends on the phone
with him as I slowly sobered up and began to regain my
regular consciousness.

The following morning, I was grateful to see daylight. It was a
dreary day, but I had never seen a more beautiful morning.
Never had I been so glad to be attacked by a spiteful
Kookaburra, and I scooped up my two ferrets, Dobby and
Niffler, for an abundance of disgustingly fragrant kisses.

I confessed to Danny that I had ignored my doctor's
diagnosis of having Bipolar 2. I was too proud a person to
accept that I had any kind of disorder. Following my trip to
rock bottom, I made the decision to seek professional help. I
found an online councillor who helped me to untangle all of
the emotional clusters I had inside me. Together, we began

finishing off my thoughts which I had been too scared to face before. I found joy once more in caring for my animals as diligently as possible, and Danny breathed a sigh of relief as he had been shouldering much of the responsibility for their care during the weeks leading up to my adventure on the bathroom floor.

My councillor, along with trusted friends and Danny, helped me to find better ways to channel both my constructive and self-destructive behaviours, and I began my journey to find out how best to live a better, healthier life. I am pleased to say that I have not felt the need to mutilate my legs for over a year, and I still gag at the sight of alcohol.

 One dream I have always had is having a dog. Many people laugh when I say this because I am so blessed to be able to share my life with a stunning variety of exotic and rescued animals. Skunks, ferrets, snakes, and hornbills,—the list is absolutely remarkable, and it almost makes my reply comical when I'm asked what my "dream" pet would be.

In my opinion, there is no love or bond like that which one can have with a dog. Their domestication has fine-tuned their ability to read us to a degree that few other animals can truly

grasp. If you ask me, the domestication of the dog is one of
humanity's greatest triumphs.

As part of my recovery to a healthier mental and physical
life, I began searching in earnest for my perfect canine
companion, deciding on the Eurasier breed. Eurasiers were
bred solely for companionship by combining some of the
most primitive breeds of dogs (Chow Chow, Wolfspitz, and
Samoyed). The result is a robust, double-coated dog which is
both rugged and regal. Their faces are a curious mix of bear,
lion, and wolf-like features, and they're typically a quiet and
extremely loyal breed.

Once I was certain that I was able to commit to a dog for the
right reasons, and once I was strong enough to understand
that dogs are never a cure for our ailments, but that they can
assist with small daily struggles, I eagerly awaited my turn on
my chosen breeder's waiting list for the right puppy for me.

Kiba, a stunning, all-black male
Eurasier was born on April 3, 2019,
many months into my personal
journey of betterment and recovery.
The breeder selected Kiba for me
from the litter as he demonstrated
the best suitability for future work
as an ESA (emotional support

animal). He was described to me as a calm, confident puppy who wasn't overbearing and who was very tuned in to his surroundings. Perfect.

There are few words to describe what it was like to have my twenty-five-year-long dream of dog companionship become a reality. My first meeting with Kiba felt like a truly auspicious affair. We clicked instantly, and he stuck by my side for much of the three days I had set aside to spend bonding with him in Nebraska before returning home to New Jersey together.

Since bringing Kiba into my life, my already much stronger mind has become even more calm and positive. No matter what my day entails, Kiba reminds me (with his extremely sharp puppy teeth) to get outside and enjoy the little things in life like discovering an insect under a leaf, playing tag, and remembering the joy of what it's like to walk in the rain.

As I write these last few words at my desk, I'm eternally grateful for the animals which make my life a truly extraordinary one. I've arrived at a place where I can appreciate the fragility of life and want to explore the endless potential that mine has. Beneath me, I can hear the soft exhalations of an otherwise silent puppy at my feet. Occasionally, he raises his head to check that I'm still close-by, and each time he catches my eye, I smile at how his usually erect ears immediately flatten to his huge, fuzzy head

in an affectionate manner, and how his curly spitz tail wags
from side to side. All that Kiba needs to be content in this
world is a little exercise, some good food, and the assurance
of lots of affection, which he always repays tenfold.

"Hi, my baby
bear," is all I
have to say for
him to open his
eyes wide and
flop onto his
side, his pink
tongue delicately
licking his black
lips as he waits for belly rubs. Sometimes I look over at my
framed picture of Bear on my desk and smile, glad that I have
the opportunity to connect myself to another soul animal.

I'm already struck by how earnest and selfless a dog's love is
for humans. Although medication should never be a source
of embarrassment or shunned where it is necessary, I am
utterly convinced that there is no medicine that can replace
the peaceful balance which comes with caring for another
creature's wellbeing and the uniquely healing love which
animals give us in their many ways.

Ferret Facts 🦦

- The Latin name for ferret is *Mustela putorius furo*, which roughly translates to "stinky little thief."

- Ferrets sometimes enter such a deep sleep that they appear completely lifeless. A ferret in this deep sleep is said to be in "dead sleep." A ferret in dead sleep can be held, tickled, and gently shaken for minutes without any sign of life.

- The grunting sounds that ferrets make when they're excited or annoyed is called "dooking."

- Baby ferrets are called "kits."

- On July 29, 1981, Princess Diana and Prince Charles's wedding was the largest televised program in history. The historical event was only able to be televised thanks to a ferret which was employed to run electrical cables through a narrow underground space beneath Buckingham Palace.

- The aviation company, Boeing, also employed ferrets to help weave cables through their aircraft. However, they stopped using ferrets quite quickly as the ferrets had a habit of falling asleep on the job.

MAGIC

A greater roadrunner swooped out from its thorny sanctuary in a cactus above a patch of parched tumbleweeds. On the ground, he paused behind a partially crumbling boulder, awkwardly slipping and stumbling over the uneven rubble. He extended his neck out from behind the decaying rocks with the air of a nosy neighbour.

Against the horizon, appearing warped and distorted in the last of the day's heat, the silhouette of a black stallion appeared, conjured from where the fuchsia sky kissed golden sand.

Magic, as he was named, was a stunning black Friesian. He walked with the swagger and confidence of an extraordinarily powerful animal, one who was fully aware that he was in his prime. He would not exercise the patience to stop for any animal in his path, neither could he be stopped by any predator in the desert, should one be foolish enough to test its luck.

A few paces ahead of Magic, an invasive stink bug was startled by the vibrations caused by the robust horse. It panicked, abandoning the shrubs it had been resting in. It blindly flew upwards, making a deep humming and clicking

sound as it whirled and zoomed in frantic motions. The
stink bug pivoted at precisely the perfect moment to find
itself plunged into the darkness of one of the magnificent
stallion's nostrils.

Surprised by this unwelcome assault, Magic halted his easy
stride and shook his head violently, snorting outwards
ferociously. His method proved to be very effective, and the
stink bug was promptly evicted. The insect unceremoniously
dropped into the sand, weighed down by a film of
mucus and dust.

"Get your head up," came an assured, amused voice from
atop the disgruntled horse. Magic corrected himself in an
instant, but still continued to grumble and snort quietly,
blowing through his nostrils.

Saddled upon his sturdy back, a cloaked and hooded figure
scanned the vast wilderness. The lone rider's face was hidden
beneath the soft, fawn-brown folds of a shemagh scarf, save
for their eyes, which were hunter focused, but also shepherd
soft and warm. Firmly in their stirrups, the rider's knee-high
riding boots were well-worn and appeared to be handcrafted.
The hooded cloak was a heavy wool garment and was a
light emerald which fell elegantly down the rider's back.
The garment was so large that when Magic would canter or

gallop, the cloak would billow dramatically behind the rider, just touching the top of the horse's jet-black tail.

The roadrunner, still spying on the imposing duo, fluffed up his crest and valiantly stood his ground, but as Magic's unyielding copper-coloured hooves marched ever closer toward the dainty bird's territory without showing any signs of changing course, he turned around in the blink of an eye and sprinted at full speed past the crumbling boulder, through the dense sea of tumbleweeds, and back up into the safety of his cactus.

As Magic and the cloaked rider effortlessly navigated the boulders, masses of thorny bushes, and scattering of fox holes, they finally came to a vast, flat expanse of desert with a mostly solid, sturdy ground and no boulders in sight. Best of all, there were three large Joshua trees.

At the sight of the Joshua trees, the rider gently leaned back and pulled slightly on the reins. Magic came to a gentle halt and listened intently.

The rider scanned the immediate area. As their head turned, so did their hands, prompting the dark horse to walk in a tight circle. The sun was beginning to dip lower, turning the sky from pink to a thunder-cloud lavender. It was here or nowhere, today.

The rider lifted their hand to their collarbone and unfastened the brass button from their wool cloak. One shoulder fell and with one strong rotation of the arm behind their neck, the rider liberated themselves from the heavy fabric and gently tossed it into a clearing. Waves of luscious, shiny black hair fell free from the confines of the hood, and a woman who looked part warrior and part elvish queen pulled the shemagh scarf from her nose and mouth.

Kimberly savoured the rapidly cooling desert air, and she filled her lungs with it as much as she could. She stretched her arms up and behind her head. Hidden beneath her huge cloak, she had been protecting one of her most prized possessions, a traditional Japanese horse bow.

Resting on her right thigh, tethered to her with a leather cord, was her hip quiver, keeping her arrows safely in place. Kimberly checked her buckles and equipment before pulling Magic around and trotting around one hundred yards away from the Joshua trees.

Magic could sense Kimberly's impending excitement. For the past two years, they had been travelling the Midwest together, strengthening their bond and learning to trust one another to create Kimberly's passion, mounted archery.

Once more, Kimberly pulled Magic back around to face
the Joshua trees, which looked like the silhouettes of angry
people shaking their fists at the sky, which was now a
pale orange.

Kimberly closed her eyes and took a deep, centring breath
as she exhaled. So too did Magic, whom she could feel was
poised and ready to accelerate at a moment's notice. She
shifted her bow and three arrows into her right hand, taking
the reins with her left. She breathed deeply once more.

"Let's go!" bellowed Kimberly, grasping the reins tightly
in her hand. By now, this was all Kimberly had to do to
communicate to her horse that he was free to work off some
of his energy. She felt Magic explode beneath her as he was
finally given permission to do what he did best—run!

The wind rushed past Kimberly's face, making whistling
sounds in her ears. Beneath her saddle, she could feel Magic's
determination to run as fast as she would permit. Dust clouds
kicked up from beneath them as they quickly entered a gallop.
For months, Kimberly's work on her mounted archery had
been with a controlled canter, but the euphoria she could feel
rising up from Magic was spellbinding. The excitement she
could feel from her beloved horse (who was every bit as wild
and untameable as she was), felt like a magnetic force driving
her forward, faster and faster.

"Come on!" she cried.

Magic didn't have to be told twice, for the first time during their mounted archery, they entered a full gallop. The first Joshua tree was coming up on her right. Kimberly leaned forward; she found her core and balance and then dropped the reins, which fell to the side of Magic's neck and shoulders.

Kimberly placed her arrow against the bow without looking— it was second nature to her now. She drew back her bow, her highly toned arms, breath, core strength, and back muscles working together in perfect unison.

She drew back her bow and let the arrow fly ahead of her. Much to Kimberly's satisfaction, the arrowhead struck the very centre of the trunk of the first Joshua tree.

Magic's rapid breathing and the howling of the wind as it whipped past them was a rush which Kimberly only felt when she rode with her horse. She had filled her life with enriching experiences over the years, from bodybuilding to starting her own business, but most feelings paled when compared to Magic. Magic was Kimberly's dream horse. She had purchased him from a man who had adored him and spent hours training him, but finally realised that he didn't have the means to care for Magic any longer.

Kimberly also had her moments of crippling self-doubt in her everyday life, but those moments didn't exist on horseback, and they couldn't reach her when she had a bow in her hand. She raised her horse bow again, this time aiming to her left and the next Joshua tree. She was going in at the side this time.

As they thundered past the tree, she turned to her side and released the arrow, sending it hurtling like a comet into a low-hanging branch of the tree. The arrow wobbled with the impact of his hit.

She whipped her body back around to focus on her next target, which lay about eighty yards ahead of her. Gripping Magic with her strong thighs as tightly as she could, Kimberly pulled back her bow and locked her eyes onto the final Joshua tree. Despite the desert rushing past her at lightning speed, Kimberly remained fixated on her target. She was ready for the big finish.

She bent forward for extra balance and pulled back the arrow as Magic continued to hurtle them toward the final target. The tree was mere feet away as they continued to rush past in a full gallop. In only a few seconds they'd be right next to the reaching branches of the Joshua tree.

Not yet!

Kimberly raised herself up from her seated position until she was suspended in a low squat. With her boots firmly in the stirrups of the saddle, Kimberly whipped her whole upper body around to the left until she was almost facing backward over her left shoulders.

They flew past the Joshua tree.

Now!

Kimberly released her arrow, but was almost beginning to lose her balance, so she whipped herself back around to concentrate on the path ahead. She grabbed up the reins and pulled back on them firmly.

"Whoa, boy," she said, slowing Magic down to a canter and then a trot.

Kimberly could feel his heavy breathing and patted him on the base of his neck to indicate to him that he'd done well. Although Magic was always enthusiastic about running and was incredibly fast, he was also a safe horse, which made activities such as mounted archery a true joy.

The beautiful palette of colours in the sky had completely faded by the time Kimberly managed to collect her cloak and scarf from the clearing where she had left them.

Her heart was still beating hard as she felt happiness and adrenaline pumping through her veins. She buttoned up her cloak and hoisted herself back up onto Magic. He was also still breathing very loudly, his nostrils flaring and closing, flaring and closing. Kimberly gently squeezed his sides with her legs and set the stallion into a trot for their journey home.

She glanced back at the very last Joshua tree and up at the glistening white arrow which she had managed to shoot up into one of its tallest branches. Above the tree, the first few stars were beginning to glisten. They seemed almost to be congratulating her.

Kimberly smiled to herself as Magic dutifully pressed onwards with their journey, exuding his ever-present confidence. She lifted her cloak's hood back over her head and pulled her scarf up under her mouth and nose.

Completely content in one another's company, the rider and stallion rode back toward the north, melting into the darkness of the desert, leaving behind nothing but a trail of moonlit hoof prints.

Horse Facts 🐎

- The teeth inside a horse's mouth takes up more space than the horse's brain.

- Horses have the largest eyes of any land mammal.

- A horse named Old Billy is thought to have been the world's longest-lived horse. Old Billy lived until he was sixty-two years old.

- Horses can sleep either standing up or lying down. When horses sleep standing up, they lock their leg joints to prevent themselves from falling over.

- Horses hooves are made of a tough protein called keratin, the same protein as our hair and nails.

- The horse's closest living relatives are the rhinoceros and the tapir.

- Fusaichi Pegasus currently holds the title for the most expensive racehorse in history. He was sold for $70 million (£53.7 million) to a racehorse stud farm in Ireland.

ACKNOWLEDGEMENTS

I've attempted to write this acknowledgement page around fifty times now, and each time I think I have it just about right, I find myself confronted with the same problem—who do I acknowledge first? So, in no particular order, please find a list of people who I am so, eternally grateful for.

From behind the scenes, I'd like to thank the wonderful *Animal Kind* team over at Mango Publishing. Shawn, Hannah, Merritt, Elina, Robin, Natasha, and Yaddyra—thank you for all of the early brainstorming meetings, for bringing your expertise to my first ever book, and for your belief in *Animal Kind*.

Also at Mango Publishing, I'd like to offer my heartfelt thanks to my editor, Hugo Villabona. Thank you for your patience while the deadline was pushed further and further back in order to afford me some space to handle extraordinary circumstances. Thank you for being so understanding, and then pulling out all of the stops to ensure that *Animal Kind* was released on schedule.

Animal Kind would absolutely not have been possible without the brilliant organizational skills of my manager, Ed Brew.

Ed, you have always been so much more than a manager. I am so fortunate to have you waving my banners even when I can't bear to wave them myself. You know so much of the struggle that went on behind the scenes as I tried my best to submit the final manuscript for *Animal Kind*. This book really wouldn't have happened with you. Thank you for being my manager, drill master, cheerleader and my friend.

Of course, I am so very grateful to Shereena K., Ragnar D., Kimberly P., and Heather F. Without the contributions of such touching, personal stories, based on real people and real animals, *Animal Kind* would not be the book it is today.

To my ever-loving and supportive family, most notably my Mummy, Daddy, Nina, and (I suppose) Toi. On the canvas of my life, you are my mountains, ever-present and always watching over me with endless love and support. I love you infinitely. And you, Toi. You're kind of okay-ish too.

My Danny—thank you for unwavering belief in me. You've lived through the creation of this book as much as I have, and I want you to know that I appreciate the little things you've done over the past few weeks, like trying to cook vitamin-rich meals for me when I hole up in my writing pit for days at a time.

Kait W.—You are one of the most beautiful souls I have ever met, and I simply could not have navigated some of these recent times without our endless phone calls which leave me crying tears of laughter.

To my second family in London—Charlie Bond (my maid of (dis)honour), you're the most feisty and loyal soul sister I could have ever hoped to have. Thank you for reminding me that it's okay to be "The Princess Who Saves Herself." You, Kelly, and Jess are some of the most wonderful support I could ever ask for and I couldn't love you three more if I tried. Khal, you're the definition of a "ride-or-die" friend. Thank you for reminding me that I am never alone.

Viewtiful Nick—I don't want to say too much and risk super-sizing that massive ego of yours, so here. Have a mention. You are...a perfectly adequate human being, and I'd just like to put it into print that I am a far superior Mario Kart Player. Thanks for proving that to be fact. Blue Shell, Nick. Blue Shell!

And finally, thank you to the animals.

Thank you for finding your way into our lives and leaving your footprints on our hearts.

ABOUT THE AUTHOR

Em is an award-winning animal educator and digital content creator. Her YouTube channel currently has over 660,000 subscribers, comprised of animal lovers and pet keepers seeking a place to learn about exotic pets and to ask questions about their care.

Her animal care and "creature feature" videos have been showcased by the BBC World Service and Blue Peter as well as many digital media outlets, such as UNILAD and LADbible. Interviews about her work as "Emzotic" have been published in newspapers and magazines such as *The Independent*, *South China Morning Post*, and *Dook Dook Ferret Magazine*.

Although born in the UK, Em spent many of her formative years in Hong Kong, catching reptiles and insects to satisfy her curiosity for nature. After returning to London and completing her formal education, Em challenged herself to find her dream career and journeyed through working as a zookeeper in London, an actress in the cult horror film *The Human Centipede 2*, and starting her own doggy day care in London's Hampstead Heath.

With conservation and creation being two of her greatest passions, Em collaborated on a honeycomb-inspired necklace with ethical jewellery company Ana Luisa. The necklace sold out worldwide in under twenty-four hours with a percentage of the profits going to bee conservation.

Having amassed a wealth of animal knowledge and living through a startling amount of extreme life experiences, Em has adopted an open-book attitude with her audience, sharing both her hard-learned lessons and her successes in the hopes that she can inspire others to embrace their passions, live courageously, and trust in their journeys.

For her work as "Emzotic," Em seeks to combine education with entertainment for her diverse audience.

Em currently lives in New Jersey along with her fiancé, bonus kids, and menagerie of animals.

Animal Kind is Em's first published work.

Mango Publishing, established in 2014, publishes an eclectic list of books by diverse authors—both new and established voices— on topics ranging from business, personal growth, women's empowerment, LGBTQ studies, health, and spirituality to history, popular culture, time management, decluttering, lifestyle, mental wellness, aging, and sustainable living. We were recently named 2019's #1 fastest growing independent publisher by *Publishers Weekly*. Our success is driven by our main goal, which is to publish high quality books that will entertain readers as well as make a positive difference in their lives.

Our readers are our most important resource; we value your input, suggestions, and ideas. We'd love to hear from you—after all, we are publishing books for you!

Please stay in touch with us and follow us at:

Facebook: Mango Publishing
Twitter: @MangoPublishing
Instagram: @MangoPublishing
LinkedIn: Mango Publishing
Pinterest: Mango Publishing

Sign up for our newsletter at www.mangopublishinggroup.com and receive a free book!

Join us on Mango's journey to reinvent publishing, one book at a time.